The poverty trade-off

The poverty trade-off

Work incentives and income redistribution in Britain

Stuart Adam, Mike Brewer and Andrew Shephard

JOSEPH ROWNTREE
FOUNDATION

First published in Great Britain in September 2006 by

The Policy Press
Fourth Floor, Beacon House
Queen's Road
Bristol BS8 1QU
UK

Tel no +44 (0)117 331 4054
Fax no +44 (0)117 331 4093
Email   tpp-info@bristol.ac.uk
www.policypress.org.uk

Published for the Joseph Rowntree Foundation by The Policy Press

10-digit ISBN 1 86134 863 0
13-digit ISBN 978 1 86134 863 0

British Library Cataloguing in Publication Data
A catalogue record for this book is available from the British Library.

Library of Congress Cataloging-in-Publication Data
A catalog record for this book has been requested.

Stuart Adam is a senior research economist, **Mike Brewer** is a programme director and
Andrew Shephard is a PhD scholar, all at the Institute for Fiscal Studies.

The **Joseph Rowntree Foundation** has supported this project as part of its programme of research and
innovative development projects, which it hopes will be of value to policy makers, practitioners and service
users. The facts presented and views expressed in this publication are, however, those of the authors and
not necessarily those of the Foundation or the Institute for Fiscal Studies.

Cover design by Qube Design Associates, Bristol
Printed in Great Britain by Latimer Trend Printing Group, Plymouth

Contents

List of tables, figures and boxes

Tables

Figures

Boxes

Acknowledgements

This report was produced as part of a project called 'Can governments reduce poverty and improve work incentives?'. The authors are very grateful to Chris Goulden, the project manager at JRF, and to the Advisory Group. Howard Reed was originally the manager of the project that led to this report, and the authors are grateful for his contributions. Material from the Family Expenditure Survey was made available by the Office for National Statistics through the UK Data Archive and has been used by permission of the Controller of HMSO. Material from the Family Resources Survey was made available by the Department for Work and Pensions, and is also available at the UK Data Archive.

Introduction

If you offer someone money on condition that they have a particular characteristic, you give them an incentive to acquire or keep that characteristic. That is the fundamental source of the trade-off between income redistribution and work incentives that confronts all governments with a dilemma.

Concern for poverty or inequality motivates governments to want to redistribute income, but providing benefits on the basis of low income reduces the incentive for people on low incomes to work themselves out of that position (over and above additional disadvantages of means-tested benefits such as stigmatising recipients, requiring burdensome form-filling and achieving less than full coverage among the entitled population). Similarly, cutting taxes on higher incomes encourages people to work to increase their income, but leaves behind those who do not do so.

Thus the two main ways for a government to help people with low incomes – providing them with support directly and encouraging them to earn more themselves – are in head-on conflict with each other. How best to deal with this conflict has long been one of the central questions facing academic economists and economic policy makers.

For academic economists, the dominant framework for thinking about how best to handle the trade-off between work incentives and redistribution is optimal taxation theory, initiated in its modern form by Mirrlees (1971). This literature attempts to specify a 'right answer' to the question – that is, a complete tax-benefit system – subject to various assumptions. However, it requires at least two vital and controversial inputs. The first is a set of social preferences: how much does society (or the government) value the additional happiness of the poor relative to the additional happiness of the rich? This is not something we know, and we did not want to assume it for this project; but without it, we can hope only to delineate the set of feasible options, not choose between them.

The second input is a set of individual preferences: most importantly, how much individuals would choose to work when faced with a given tax and benefit system. Some models attempt to estimate this based on individuals' responses to past tax and benefit changes: see Brewer et al (2005) for a recent example. But all such estimates remain controversial and laden with assumptions, and we do not espouse any here.

In this project, therefore, we estimate only the direct effects of policies on incomes and on work incentives; we ignore any effect that people's responses to these changed work incentives might have on incomes. As a result, we cannot judge whether, for example, the weakening of work incentives caused by a particular redistributive policy will draw more people into poverty than the redistribution itself lifts out. This report aims to illuminate the trade-off between work incentives and redistribution, not to predict the ultimate outcomes associated with policy choices or assess their desirability.

This project has three aims:

(1) to evaluate various techniques of quantifying the financial incentives to work;

(2) to analyse how financial work incentives have changed across the population in Britain since 1979, and to estimate how much of these changes are due to changes in the tax and benefit system;

(3) to quantify the trade-off between redistributing income and strengthening work incentives, both by examining historical trends and by simulating plausible hypothetical changes to the tax and benefit system in 2005–06.

The first two of these are covered in detail in Adam et al (2006); this report summarises that and explores the third point in detail.

Different governments, politicians and commentators have taken different stances on the redistribution–work incentives trade-off. In practice, a straightforward dichotomy between two competing approaches is too simplistic: governments have a great deal of scope for precise management of the trade-off beyond simply choosing a point on a generic scale from 'no redistribution, excellent work incentives' to 'full redistribution, no work incentives'. For example, by changing the rate at which benefits are withdrawn with income they can move between a situation in which a few people face very weak work incentives and one in which lots of people face quite weak work incentives. Or by providing support to low-income people in work, they can achieve some redistribution (although not to the poorest, who tend to be out of work) and provide an incentive to move into work (although weakening the incentive to increase earnings once in work). Chapter 5 examines in detail the effect of these and other kinds of reform on the distributions of income and work incentives.

How severe the trade-off between work incentives and redistribution seems can depend on how strictly limited the government's resources are. A government with money 'to spare' can reduce poverty without weakening work incentives by giving *everyone* money, helping those on low incomes while maintaining the differential that provides work incentives. For any given level of resources, of course, the trade-off is still there: the same amount of money could do more to reduce poverty if it were targeted on the basis of low income, or more to strengthen work incentives if it were restricted to people in work or on higher incomes. But spending more allows governments to achieve a better combination of work incentives and redistribution. Thus in the short term we can discern a three-way trade-off between redistribution, work incentives and government costs: this has been called the 'iron triangle' of welfare reform (Blundell, 2002). In the long run, however, the third dimension disappears. Money given to people now that is not taken from other people now can only be funded by borrowing, which means making everyone worse off again when the debt is repaid. So simply spending more money to soften the trade-off between redistribution and disincentives now can only be done by weakening the trade-off that must be faced in the future.

The trade-off between redistribution and work incentives is not wholly inescapable, however, because 'support targeted at poor people' need not necessarily mean 'support conditional on being poor'. An alternative approach to redistribution involves making support conditional on *correlates* of poverty (typically demographic characteristics) rather than on measures of poverty itself. For example, if people who are old, disabled or have lots of children are disproportionately likely to be poor, then providing support on the basis of old age, disability or number of children can achieve substantial redistribution while limiting disincentives to work. This approach is known in the optimal taxation literature as 'tagging', following Akerlof (1978).[1] In practice it typically takes the form of 'categorical' benefits, such as child benefit and disability living allowance in the UK.

---

[1] Strictly, tagging refers not only to the provision of non-means-tested transfers to particular groups, but more generally to the application of different tax and benefit schedules to groups with different characteristics. However, in this report we look only at the former.

Tagging has drawbacks. It inevitably involves targeting the poor less accurately than using direct measures of poverty: since no characteristic is perfectly correlated with poverty, tagging will always fail to reach some poor people while providing 'unneeded' support for some better-off people. Furthermore, irrespective of its efficiency or otherwise in targeting poverty, some would argue that it is fundamentally unfair to discriminate in favour of certain demographic groups in this way (membership of certain minority ethnic groups is an excellent predictor of poverty, but there is little prospect of any government introducing a 'black person's benefit', for example). A third difficulty with tagging is implied by the opening sentence of this Introduction: offering money conditional on *any* characteristic provides people with an incentive to acquire or keep that characteristic. Tagging does not simply remove incentive problems: rather, it replaces one incentive (the incentive to remain poor) with another (the incentive to have whatever 'tag' is used to proxy poverty). How far people are likely to respond to this incentive will depend on what the tag is: it is hard to envisage people responding to an incentive to be old, but they might respond to an incentive to have more children; they are unlikely to make themselves (more) disabled, but they might be tempted to pretend they are less healthy than they really are. Other things being equal, such distortions of behaviour are undesirable; how to balance them against the disincentives to work created by traditional redistribution packages is an issue policy makers must address.

In Chapter 5 we analyse examples of tagging. But in this report we restrict ourselves to analysing work incentives and the income distribution: we do not look at other incentives created by the tax and benefit system, nor at other aspects of perceived 'fairness'. Thus the merits or otherwise of tagging are not the focus of the report, and the findings on tagging policies in Chapter 5 reflect only the first of the three difficulties described above.

The rest of the report is structured as follows:

Chapter 2 explains how we measure financial work incentives. In Chapter 3, we show how they vary across the population in 2005–06 and how they have changed since 1979. Previous work has examined how the current Labour government's tax and benefit reforms have altered work incentives for parents since 1997 (Brewer and Clark, 2002; Brewer and Shephard, 2004), but this is the first attempt to examine trends over a much longer period or to decompose the trends in such detail. We also attempt a decomposition analysis that tells us to what extent the changes in work incentives are attributable to changes in the tax and benefit system, to changes in real earnings, and to changes in the demographic make-up of the population and other factors. A companion paper, Adam et al (2006), presents our results in more detail.

Much is already known about trends in poverty and inequality in the UK, and about how tax and benefit reforms have contributed to those trends. DWP (2006) and Brewer et al (2006c) describe the income distribution now, and Jones (2005) describes how it is affected by taxes and benefits. Looking over time, Clark and Leicester (2004) and Goodman et al (1997) all attempt to quantify the effect of tax and benefit reforms on inequality, while Dickens and Ellwood (2003), Sutherland et al (2003) and Brewer et al (2003) look at how reforms have affected child poverty under the current government. Chapter 4 brings this literature together with the new analysis in Chapter 3 to explore the historical link between inequality and poverty and financial work incentives in Britain.

Chapter 5 takes a different approach to quantifying the trade-off: looking at options available to the current government. We simulate the impact of a variety of possible changes to taxes and benefits in 2005–06, and compare their effects on work incentives and the income distribution.

Chapter 6 concludes.

Much of our analysis is based on measures of net incomes and work incentives produced by the Institute for Fiscal Studies' tax and benefit micro-simulation model, TAXBEN, and the Appendix gives full details of our approach.

2

Measuring financial work incentives

This chapter defines some important measures of financial work incentives, and discusses a number of detailed issues involved when measuring financial work incentives using a micro-simulation model. More detail is in the Appendix and in Adam et al (2006).

An individual's financial incentive to work will depend on the shape of the relationship between hours of paid work and net income, taking account of the financial costs of working and not working.[2] This relationship is known as a 'budget constraint': see Figure 2.1a for an example. Budget constraints tell us all we might want to know about the financial incentives for an individual to work, but it is often preferable to summarise this information in some convenient measure. In doing this, there are two important dimensions of the budget constraint that we attempt to quantify:

- the financial reward for working compared with not working, measured by some function of incomes in and out of work, which we call the **incentive to work at all**;
- the incentive for those already in work to work harder or earn more, which we call the **incentive to progress** in the labour market.

Two common measures of the incentive to work at all are the replacement rate and the participation tax rate:

- The **replacement rate** is measured by (net income out of work)/(net income in work). For example, if someone received £50 in benefits if they did not work, and had a net income of £200 if they worked, then the replacement rate is 50/200 or 0.25.
- The **participation tax rate** is measured by 1 – ([net income in work – net income out of work]/gross earnings), or one minus the financial gain to working as a proportion of gross earnings. It measures the proportion of gross earnings taken in tax or reduced benefits. To continue the previous example, if that person had gross earnings of £250, then the participation tax rate would be 1 – (200 – 50)/250, or 0.4.

Low numbers of both mean stronger financial incentives to work: a participation tax rate of zero would mean that an individual got to keep all of their gross earnings, and lost no benefits or tax credits, when they worked; a replacement rate of zero occurs where someone has no income if they do not work. At the other extreme, a participation tax rate or a replacement rate of 1 would mean that there is no financial reward to working. High participation tax rates or replacement rates are often referred to as the unemployment trap.

These measures are different, and behave differently following different sorts of changes in income. In general, the replacement rate better captures the strength of the incentive to work at all, while the participation tax rate better captures how government policy

---

[2] 'Net income' means income after benefits and tax credits have been added and after direct taxes have been deducted.

(through the tax and benefit system) affects the incentive to work. Furthermore, the two measures can give very different impressions of the incentive to work faced by adults in couples. More information is given in Box 2.1.

The incentive for those in work to progress in the labour market can be measured by the **effective marginal tax rate** (EMTR), the slope of the budget constraint. The EMTR measures how much of a small change in earnings is lost to direct tax payments and foregone state benefit and tax credit entitlements, and it tells us about the strength of the incentive for individuals to increase their earnings slightly, whether through working more hours, or through promotion, qualifying for bonus payments or getting a better-paid job. In this report, we use the term 'incentives to progress' for all these possibilities.

As with the incentive to work at all, low numbers mean stronger financial incentives. An EMTR of zero means that the individual keeps all of any small change in earnings, and a rate of 1 (or 100%) means that the individual keeps none (high EMTRs among workers in low-income families are often referred to as a poverty trap).

All these standard work-incentive measures can be derived from a standard budget constraint diagram. The four figures below show the relationship between the budget constraint (the relationship between hours worked and net income) and the three main measures of work incentives discussed here. Figure 2.1a shows a hypothetical budget constraint (for a lone parent with one child aged three, earning £6 an hour, with no savings income, no housing costs, no financial costs of working, no formal childcare costs, an average [England and Wales] Band D council tax liability, under the April 2005 tax and benefit system).

The EMTR – our measure of incentives to progress in the labour market – is the slope of this line, and is shown in Figure 2.1b. EMTRs of 100% occur when an individual is entitled to income support and every £1 of private earnings above the disregard reduces the income support payment by £1.

Figures 2.1c and 2.1d show the two measures of the financial incentive to work at all: the replacement rate (2.1c) and the participation tax rate (2.1d). The dotted lines on Figure 2.1a show how these are calculated for someone working 16 hours a week. This person would have gross earnings of a, would receive b in benefits if they did not work, and would have a net income of c if they worked 16 hours. The formula for the replacement rate at 16 hours is b/c, and the formula for the participation tax rate is $1 - (c - b)/a$.

These are discussed in full in Adam et al (2006), and the Appendix sets out how we calculate work incentives in the analysis in this report.

Figure 2.1a: A budget constraint for a lone parent with one child, April 2005 tax and benefit system

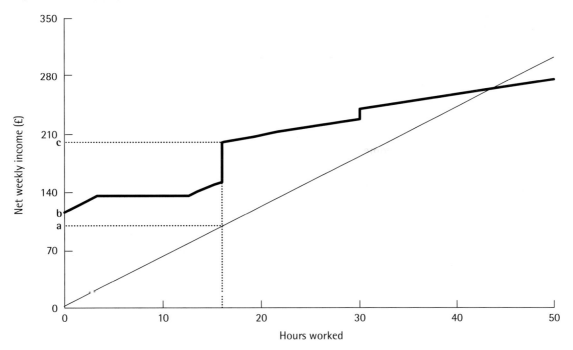

Notes and sources: a and c are the levels of gross earnings and net income respectively for this person if they work 16 hours, and b is their net income (from benefits) if they do not work. Authors' calculations using TAXBEN under April 2005 tax and benefit system. See text for details of corresponding example family type.

Figure 2.1b: An example of how EMTRs vary with hours worked

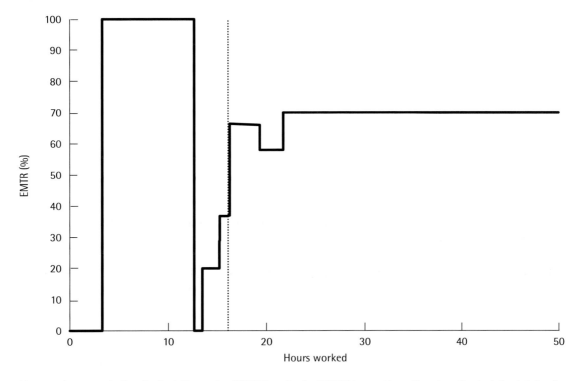

Notes and sources: Authors' calculations using TAXBEN under April 2005 tax and benefit system. See text for details of corresponding example family type.

Figure 2.1c: An example of how replacement rates vary with hours worked

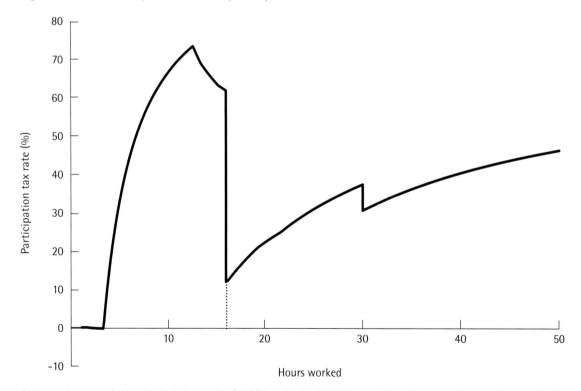

Notes and sources: Authors' calculations using TAXBEN under April 2004 tax and benefit system. See text for details of corresponding example family type.

Figure 2.1d: An example of how the participation tax rate varies with hours worked

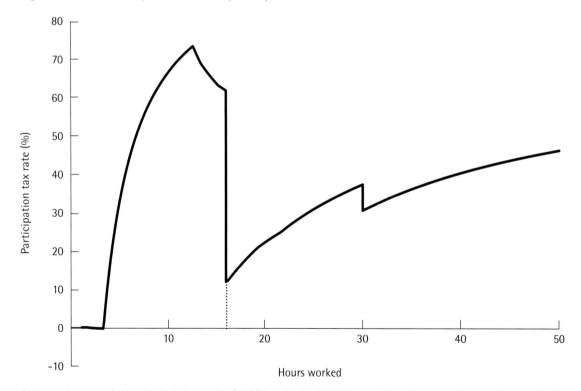

Notes and sources: Authors' calculations using TAXBEN under April 2004 tax and benefit system. See text for details of corresponding example family type.

3

Financial work incentives in Britain: 1979 to 2005

This chapter presents an overview of financial work incentives for people working in Britain in 2005, showing what types of people tend to face strong or weak financial work incentives. We then summarise what we know about changes in work incentives since 1979. As well as showing the main trends, we show to what extent the changes can be explained by various factors, such as changes to the tax and benefit system, changes in the real level of wages and their distribution, and changes to the real level of rents. Much more detail can be found in Adam et al (2006). A key limitation is that our analysis is restricted to individuals who are employees, are aged under 55 and are not receiving a disability benefit.

Work incentives in 2005

The distribution of replacement rates among working adults is shown in Table 3.1. The most common range of replacement rates faced by these adults in 2005 is between 50% and 60%, where around 2.75 million adults are located (this means that these adults' families would receive 50–60% of their current income if the individual stopped work). Almost 70% of individuals face replacement rates between 20% and 70%, and the distribution of replacement rates is roughly symmetric: there is a similar number of

Table 3.1: Replacement rates among working adults

%	Number of working adults with rate in this band	Number who face rate in or higher than this band
0	50,000	17,800,000
0.1–10	470,000	17,740,000
10.1–20	1,640,000	17,270,000
20.1–30	2,400,000	15,630,000
30.1–40	2,180,000	13,230,000
40.1–50	2,640,000	11,050,000
50.1–60	2,750,000	8,410,000
60.1–70	2,100,000	5,660,000
70.1–80	1,690,000	3,560,000
80.1–90	1,270,000	1,870,000
90.1–100	560,000	600,000
Over 100	40,000	40,000
All	17,800,000	

Notes and sources: Authors' calculations using Family Resources Survey 2002–03 and TAXBEN under April 2005 tax and benefit system. See Appendix for detail of sample. Excludes adults aged over 55, the self-employed, adults receiving a disability benefit and other adults living in these families. Figures grossed up using FRS weights and rounded to nearest 10,000. Numbers may not add because of rounding.

people with very high replacement rates (weak work incentives) as with very low replacement rates (strong work incentives).

Among the population as a whole, there are several factors that lead to this variation in replacement rates: individuals could be facing high replacement rates if they have a low wage, only work a few hours every week, or if the tax and benefit system means that they face high levels of out-of-work income. Understanding the variation in replacements rates is much more straightforward when examining the incentives within different family groups, because most of the variation in replacement rates within family groups is derived from variation in wages.

Table 3.2 shows that the most common participation tax rate band is between 30% and 40%, with 5.1 million individuals facing rates in this range. Unlike the distribution of replacement rates, the distribution of participation tax rates is positively skewed.

Table 3.3 shows the distribution of effective marginal tax rates (EMTRs).[3] This distribution has a large spike at tax rates of between 30% and 40%: nearly two thirds of working adults have EMTRs in this range. This can be easily understood in terms of the parameters of the tax and benefit system: the single most common EMTR faced by workers under the April 2005 tax and benefit system is 33%, the rate that applies to adults whose own earnings are high enough to pay basic-rate income tax, but lower than the upper earnings limit in national insurance, who are contracted into the state second pension, and with a family income sufficiently high that they have no entitlements to means-tested benefits or tax credits (beyond the family element of the child tax credit).

Table 3.2: Participation tax rates among working adults

%	Number of working adults with rate in this band	Number who face rate in or higher than this band
0	500,000	17,800,000
0.1–10	570,000	17,320,000
10.1–20	1,450,000	16,750,000
20.1–30	4,490,000	15,300,000
30.1–40	4,610,000	10,810,000
40.1–50	2,870,000	6,200,000
50.1–60	1,610,000	3,330,000
60.1–70	850,000	1,720,000
70.1–80	520,000	870,000
80.1–90	260,000	350,000
90.1–100	50,000	90,000
Over 100	40,000	40,000
All	17,800,000	

Notes and sources: Authors' calculations using Family Resources Survey 2002–03 and TAXBEN under April 2005 tax and benefit system. Excludes families containing any adults aged over 55, the self-employed, or adults receiving a disability benefit. Figures grossed up using FRS weights and rounded to nearest 10,000. Numbers may not add because of rounding.

---

[3] Table 4.2 of HM Treasury (2006) shows similar estimates. The key differences between the two tables are that: (a) the Treasury's estimates only apply to people working at least 16 hours a week; ours apply to anyone working any hours; (b) the Treasury's estimates count the number of families; ours count the number of workers; (c) the Treasury's estimates incorporate some non-take-up of tax credits and means-tested benefits; ours assume full take-up.

Table 3.3: EMTRs among working adults

%	Number of working adults with rate in this band	Number who face rate in or higher than this band
0	560,000	17,800,000
0.1–10	110,000	17,240,000
10.1–20	250,000	17,130,000
20.1–30	1,640,000	16,880,000
30.1–40	10,900,000	15,240,000
40.1–50	2,130,000	4,340,000
50.1–60	240,000	2,210,000
60.1–70	1,390,000	1,970,000
70.1–80	180,000	580,000
80.1–90	240,000	400,000
90.1–100	120,000	160,000
Over 100	40,000	40,000
All	17,800,000	

Notes and sources: Authors' calculations using Family Resources Survey 2002–03 and TAXBEN under April 2005 tax and benefit system. Excludes families containing any adults aged over 55, the self-employed, or adults receiving a disability benefit. Figures grossed up using FRS weights and rounded to nearest 10,000. Numbers may not add because of rounding. EMTRs calculated by increasing hours of work by 5%.

EMTRs of 20% or below – which apply to just under 5% of working adults – are faced by low-earning adults who earn too little to pay basic-rate income tax, and who live either in families who are too rich to be subject to withdrawal of in-work support (because they live with a high-earning partner) or in families whose joint income is sufficiently low so that the adults are not subject to a withdrawal of means-tested benefits or tax credits (in other words, these are low-earning individuals in either very low-income or relative high-income families).

EMTRs between 40% and 50% – which is the second most common range of marginal tax rates – tend to apply to adults who earn enough to pay the higher rate of income tax. EMTRs beyond this – and there are around 2.2 million workers who face EMTRs in excess of 50% – almost always arise when adults live in a family whose income means that they face a withdrawal of a means-tested benefit or a tax credit. Indeed, the highest EMTRs arise when adults are eligible for more than one means-tested benefit or tax credit, usually housing benefit or council tax benefit in conjunction with tax credits: in April 2005, an individual facing simultaneous withdrawal of tax credits and housing benefit as well as basic-rate income tax and standard-rate national insurance contributions (NICs) would face an effective marginal tax rate of 89.5% – or 95.5% if they also faced withdrawal of council tax benefit. Most working adults in receipt of income support are subject to a 100% marginal tax rate, as every £1 of private earnings above the small disregard is wholly offset by a £1 reduction in their income support entitlement.

How do work incentives in 2005 vary by family type?

The previous section examined the distribution of work incentives across the working population; this section shows how incentives vary by family type.

Table 3.4: Financial work incentives of working adults in different family types, April 2005

	RR	PTR	EMTR
Single adults without children			
Mean	33.9	46.8	35.1
Median	25.9	39.6	33.0
25th centile	18.7	35.8	31.4
75th centile	37.6	50.0	33.0
Men in couples without children			
Mean	43.0	29.0	33.8
Median	43.2	26.8	33.0
25th centile	33.8	23.9	31.4
75th centile	51.7	31.8	33.0
Women in couples without children			
Mean	59.6	22.3	31.1
Median	58.5	22.1	31.4
25th centile	50.0	17.0	31.4
75th centile	68.8	25.4	33.0
Lone parents			
Mean	64.2	33.8	56.7
Median	64.3	45.1	68.4
25th centile	50.2	21.8	33.0
75th centile	79.7	56.0	70.0
Men in couples with children			
Mean	52.4	45.2	42.0
Median	52.1	42.7	33.8
25th centile	41.2	34.4	31.4
75th centile	63.9	54.3	47.1
Women in couples with children			
Mean	72.6	23.4	33.0
Median	73.9	23.2	33.0
25th centile	62.9	13.0	31.4
75th centile	82.9	33.5	37.0
All			
Mean	49.4	36.6	36.4
Median	48.5	35.4	33.0
25th centile	29.5	25.5	31.4
75th centile	65.4	45.5	39.1

Notes and sources: Authors' calculations using Family Resources Survey 2002–03 and TAXBEN under April 2005 tax and benefit system. Excludes families containing any adults aged over 55, the self-employed, or adults receiving a disability benefit. EMTR calculated by increasing hours of work by 5%. RR = replacement rate. PTR = participation tax rate. EMTR = effective marginal tax rate.

Table 3.4 shows the mean, median and quartile points of replacement rates, participation tax rates and effective marginal tax rates for people in six different family types:[4]

- single adults without children[5]
- men and women (separately) in couples without children
- lone parents
- men and women (separately) in couples with children.

---

4   The median (50th centile) is the middle number, such that half of individuals have higher replacement rates (say) than this and half have lower. Similarly, the first quartile (25th centile) is the number that 25% of replacement rates are below, and the third quartile (75th centile) is the number that 75% of replacement rates are below.

5   'Children' means 'dependent children'.

The financial work incentives of these groups are very different. Lone parents face some of the weakest incentives to work at all, and face weak incentives to progress in the labour market. They face weak incentives to progress because many working lone parents will be subject to withdrawal of a tax credit or means-tested benefit as their earnings rise. For the same reason, and because of the low average wage that they receive and high levels of out-of-work income, they face weak incentives to work at all.

Meanwhile, single adults without children face some of the strongest incentives to progress. The relatively low level of state support that is provided to these people when they are not working means that their replacement rates are generally low. The incentive to progress is relatively strong for this group, with most individuals being subject just to the basic rate of income tax and NICs. The incentive to progress is weaker for high-wage individuals who pay the higher rate of income tax, and also for very low-earning individuals who may be receiving a means-tested benefit or working tax credit.

The table gives a mixed impression about the incentive to progress for people in couples. Looking at men in couples first, it can be seen that those who live in families with children have a weaker incentive to progress than those who do not. This is partly because men who live in couples with dependent children tend to be older, and so are more likely to be subject to the higher rate of income tax and therefore face a higher EMTR. Furthermore, they are much more likely to be subject to tax credit withdrawal. Men in couples with dependent children also face a weaker incentive to work at all (measured by both the replacement rate and the participation tax rate) than those without, because those with children would usually be entitled to tax credits even if no one in the family is working.

A similar pattern exists for women in couples: those in families with dependent children tend to face higher EMTRs and higher replacement rates than those in families with no dependent children. However, an important feature of the work incentives faced by women in couples is the different impressions given by the replacement rate and the participation tax rate: incentives to work at all appear quite weak when considering the replacement rate, but seem relatively strong when considering the participation tax rate. This is because women in couples are much more likely than men to have working (and high-earning) partners, and so the decision to work of a woman in a couple – especially if part time or for a relatively low wage – may make little difference to family income, while these small additional earnings may be subject to little income tax or NICs, and may make no difference to the family's tax credit entitlement.

Changes in work incentives over time

This section summarises what we know about changes in work incentives since 1979. We first show the main trends, and then illustrate how much of the changes can be explained by various factors, such as changes to the tax and benefit system, changes in the real level of wages and their distribution, and changes to the real level of rents.

The incentive to work at all

The financial incentive to work at all, as captured by both the replacement rate and the participation tax rate, has generally strengthened (that is, fallen) between 1979 and 2005: see Figures 3.1 and 3.2. These and later figures show five series over time: the 10th, 25th, 50th, 75th and 90th centiles of the distribution of work incentives within a particular group of the population. The 10th and 25th centiles illustrate the financial work incentives of people with relatively strong financial work incentives, and the 75th and 90th centiles illustrate the incentives of people with relatively weak financial work incentives.

Figures 3.1 and 3.2 show that incentives to work at all:

- are stronger in 2005 than in 1979, on average;
- weakened in the early 1980s, at the turn of the 1990s, and in the early 2000s;
- weakened over most of the 1980s and over most of the 1990s;
- got more dispersed over time when measured by the replacement rate, but less dispersed when measured by the participation tax rate.

The incentive to progress

Trends in the financial incentive to progress – as measured by EMTRs – are shown in Figure 3.3.

- The economy-wide median incentive shows a similar pattern to the incentive to work at all. It weakened in the early 1980s, and strengthened rapidly between 1985 and 1988. Between 1988 and 1995, it weakened slightly, then strengthened between 1995 and 1997, since when it has been weakening once more.
- The distribution of incentives to progress has become much more dispersed over time: in 1979, 80% of the population faced EMTRs of between 29% and 37%; in 2005/06, the range is between 23% and 68%. The strongest incentives to progress (measured by the 10th centile) have strengthened by more than the median, particularly between 1995 and 2000, when tax rates for low earners were being cut, and the weakest incentives to progress (measured by the 90th centile) have got a lot weaker since 1999, as eligibility for in-work support extended both up the income distribution and (in 2003) to people without children.

Figure 3.1: Replacement rates (1979–2005)

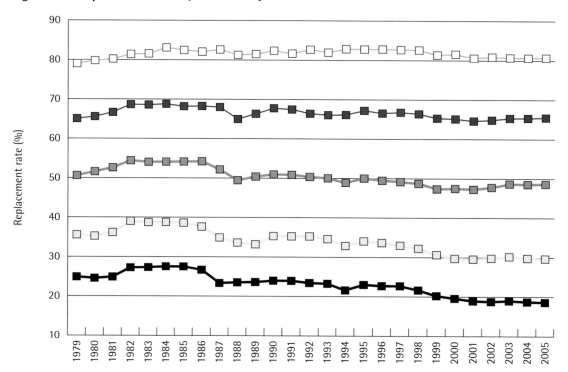

Notes and sources: Authors' calculations using various years of Family Expenditure Survey/Family Resources Survey 2002–03 and TAXBEN. Excludes families containing any adults aged over 55, the self-employed, or adults receiving a disability benefit. Replacement rates evaluated at usual hours worked. Figure shows, from bottom to top, the changes in the 10th, 25th, 50th, 75th and 90th centiles of the distribution.

Figure 3.2: Participation tax rates (1979–2005)

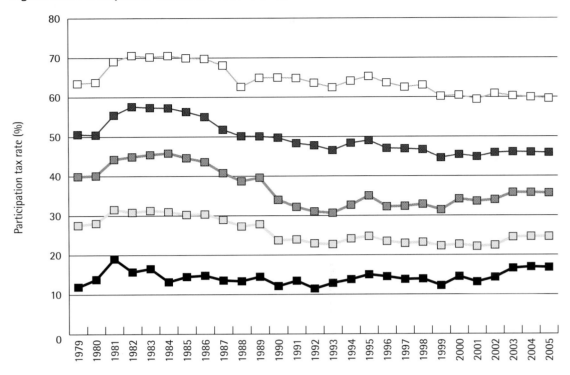

Notes and sources: Authors' calculations using various years of Family Expenditure Survey/Family Resources Survey 2002–03 and TAXBEN. Excludes families containing any adults aged over 55, the self-employed, or adults receiving a disability benefit. Replacement rates evaluated at usual hours worked. Figure shows, from bottom to top, the changes in the 10th, 25th, 50th, 75th and 90th centiles of the distribution.

Figure 3.3: EMTRs (1979–2005)

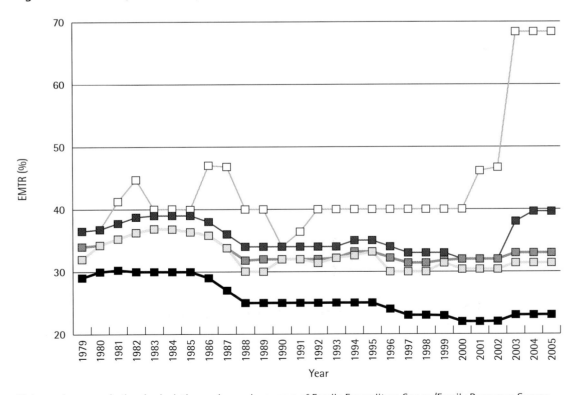

Notes and sources: Authors' calculations using various years of Family Expenditure Survey/Family Resources Survey 2002–03 and TAXBEN. Excludes families containing any adults aged over 55, the self-employed, or adults receiving a disability benefit. Replacement rates evaluated at usual hours worked. Figure shows, from bottom to top, the changes in the 10th, 25th, 50th, 75th and 90th centiles of the distribution.

- Since 2003, more than one in four workers have faced an effective marginal tax rate of around 40% or more, the first time this has happened since 1985. This reflects both the impact of fiscal drag on the number of higher-rate taxpayers and the increasing numbers of workers entitled to in-work support.[6]

These changes in work incentives could be due to changes in tax and benefit systems, wage rates, working patterns and anything else affecting individuals' budget constraints. Decomposition analysis seeks to isolate the contributions of various factors – such as changes in the tax and benefit system, wages, rents, and the demographic make-up of the population – to the changes over time (see Box 3.1 for the precise details). Our analysis (see Adam et al, 2006) shows that:

- Real wage growth has greatly strengthened the incentive to work at all (measured by replacement rates), because out-of-work benefits have typically been increased only in line with price inflation, not average wage growth. Growth in real wages has had virtually no net effect on the average incentive to progress: real wage growth should mean that the number of adults eligible for means-tested benefits or tax credits falls, but that the number who pay higher-rate income tax rises, and these have offsetting impacts on the average incentive to progress.
- The cumulative effect of 26 years of real tax and benefit changes has been to strengthen work incentives. The pattern has not been even, however: between 1979 and 1983, real tax and benefit changes tended to weaken the incentive to work; between 1983 and the late 1990s, they tended to strengthen it; and the most recent changes have tended to weaken it once more. Since 1999, tax and benefit changes have increased the average EMTR by almost three percentage points.
- Increased wage inequality, increased real rents and all other changes have all weakened the incentive to work at all and the incentive to progress, on average.

Changes in work incentives for different groups

The project looked in detail at how different groups' work incentives have changed over time. We found that:

- *the incentive for lone parents to work part-time* (compared with not working) is generally stronger now than in 1979, both because real wages have risen and because in-work support is now available for part-time as well as full-time workers. On the other hand, real rent rises and housing benefit have weakened the incentive for lone parents to work, and incentives to work in 2005 are slightly weaker than they were in 1999.
- By extending in-work support to many more lone parents, reforms to family credit in the early 1990s mean that *incentives to progress for lone parents* are weaker now than they were in 1979, on average, for those already in work. In more recent years, the expansion of tax credits has increased EMTRs for relatively well-off lone parents previously facing strong incentives to progress, but the cut in the withdrawal rate to in-work benefits in 1999 strengthened some of the worst incentives to progress. But it is still the case in 2005/06 that more than half of working lone parents would, once the temporary disregard in tax credits expires, keep less than a third of any extra earnings if they worked an hour or two more each week.

---

[6] People rich enough to pay higher-rate tax but who are contracted out of the state second pension would face an EMTR of 39.4% after April 2003 (we ignore the additional age-related NICs rebate that applies to people who are contracted out into defined contribution pension schemes).

Box 3.1: Understanding the changes in financial work incentives through a decomposition analysis

The main technique used in our work to understand the changes in financial work incentives is to decompose the observed changes into those caused by changes to the tax and benefit system, and those due to changes in the characteristics of the working population.

To do this, we start with the population observed in 1979 facing the tax and benefit system of 1979. We then change economic variables and characteristics of this population until we end up with the actual population in a different year (say 2000), with the actual tax and benefit system of 2000.[7] The stages in the decomposition are described below, assuming for simplicity that we are only comparing 1979 and 2000 (in reality we do this for every year):

(1) Identify the contribution of changes in the level and distribution of wages, by assuming that the population in 2000 has the same real characteristics as in 1979 except for wages, which follow the distribution of the 2000 population. We do this by projecting the actual wage distribution in 2000 onto the 1979 population, so that each 1979 individual is assigned the wage of someone observed in 2000 with the same wage ranking within the relevant demographic group.

(2) Identify the additional contribution of real changes in average rents (but still assuming that the proportion of the group in rented accommodation is the same as in 1979) by increasing all rents by the growth in average rents between 1979 and 2000.

(3) Identify the additional contribution of real changes to the tax and benefit system by allowing the tax and benefit system to change.[8]

(4) Identify the additional contribution of all other changes that might affect financial work incentives, such as changes in non-earned income, housing tenure, local taxes, disability and ill-health, and, among parents, the number and age of dependent children, and changes in the working patterns among couples.

It is important to recognise that decompositions have limitations. At best, they capture only the direct effect of policy: they show what poverty, inequality and work incentives would have looked like in the absence of policy changes, holding all other factors constant. But in practice people may well have behaved differently if different policies had been in place, and so this decomposition approach cannot tell us, for example, how far tax and benefit changes reduced poverty by encouraging people to move into work.

---

[7] Similar analyses have been undertaken by, for example, Adam and Brewer (2004) to explain changes in child-contingent support, and Dickens and Ellwood (2004) to explain changes in child poverty in the US and UK.

[8] When looking at changes over this long period (25 years), it is arguably more sensible to assume that the appropriate index for uprating tax and benefit parameters over time should be the growth in average earnings rather than the growth in average retail prices (see Clark and Leicester, 2004; Evans and Eyre, 2004). However, we have decided to assume that 'no real changes' is the baseline, but to show the impact of real changes in the tax and benefit system separately from the impact of real changes in wages.

- Growth in real earnings led to a gradual strengthening of *the incentive to be in work for men and women in couples with children* from the early 1980s to the late 1990s, but tax and benefit changes weakened incentives to work both before and after this period.

- Higher earnings among working mothers have meant that more of them now pay income tax than in 1979, dulling incentives to progress. Aside from this, the main change to *incentives to progress for adults in couples with children* has taken place since the late 1990s, with the expansion of in-work support weakening incentives to progress for a minority.

- *Single adults without children faced relatively strong incentives to be in work even in 1979.* Real wage growth since then has strengthened this further, as have tax and benefit changes.

- *Incentives to progress for single adults without children* strengthened for most of the period, but weakened in the early 1980s, and have been getting weaker since the late 1990s: these changes are driven by real tax and benefit changes.

- For both *men and women in couples without children*, the tax and benefit systems of the early and mid-1980s had weaker incentives (both the incentive to work and to progress) than those of the 1990s and 2000s. Growth in wages, particularly for women in couples without children, has also been very important in explaining the strengthening of the incentive to work at all. But the work incentives inherent in the tax and benefit system of 2005 are generally weaker than they were in 1999.

4

Poverty, inequality and work incentives over time

Chapter 1 discussed in general terms the trade-off that arises between work incentives and redistribution of income. In this chapter, we look at how far this trade-off has been visible in broad aggregate measures of work incentives and the income distribution since 1979.

Figures 4.1, 4.2 and 4.3 all show the levels of poverty and inequality (according to particular definitions – see Box 4.1) since 1979. Alongside these levels are shown the mean and median replacement rates (Figure 4.1), participation tax rates (Figure 4.2) and effective marginal tax rates (EMTRs) (Figure 4.3) among workers.

The poverty and inequality measures are highly correlated with all of the work incentive measures: average work incentives have tended to be strongest in years when poverty and inequality have been highest. These correlations range from –0.51 (between the mean replacement rate and the poverty rate) to –0.89 (between the median EMTR and

Figure 4.1: Poverty, inequality and replacement rates (1979–2005)

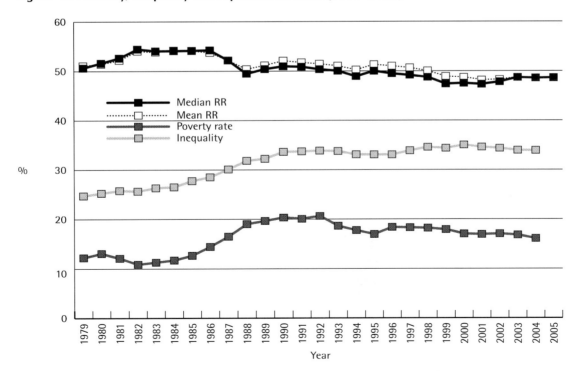

Notes and sources: Authors' calculations using various years of Family Expenditure Survey/Family Resources Survey 2002–03 and TAXBEN, and official Households Below Average Income data. Replacement rates evaluated at usual hours worked and exclude families containing any adults aged over 55, the self-employed, or adults receiving a disability benefit. RR = replacement rate.

Figure 4.2: Poverty, inequality and participation tax rates (1979–2005)

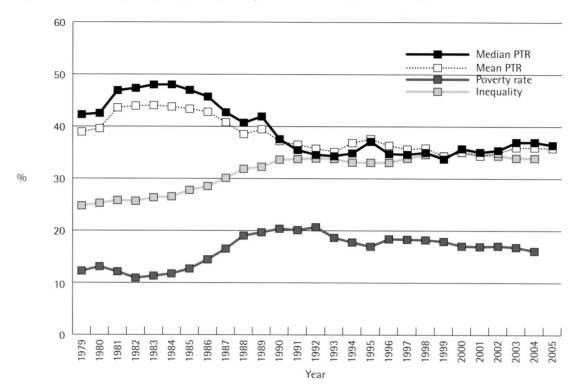

Notes and sources: Authors' calculations using various years of Family Expenditure Survey/Family Resources Survey 2002–03 and TAXBEN, and official Households Below Average Income data. Participation tax rates evaluated at usual hours worked and exclude families containing any adults aged over 55, the self-employed, or adults receiving a disability benefit. PTR = participation tax rate.

Figure 4.3: Poverty, inequality and EMTRs (1979–2005)

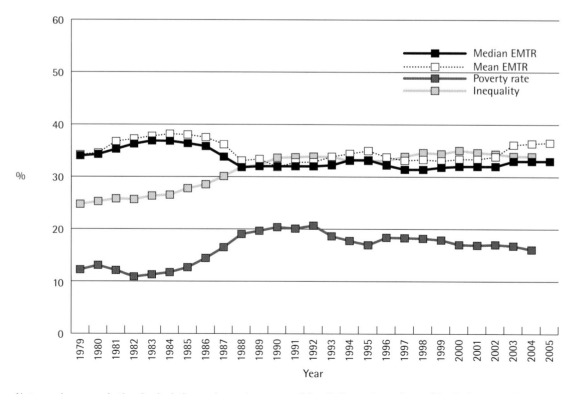

Notes and sources: Authors' calculations using various years of Family Expenditure Survey/Family Resources Survey 2002–03 and TAXBEN, and official Households Below Average Income data. EMTRs evaluated at usual hours worked and exclude families containing any adults aged over 55, the self-employed, or adults receiving a disability benefit.

Box 4.1: Measures of poverty and inequality

The many ways to measure poverty and inequality have been discussed extensively elsewhere. In this chapter, we simply adopt one commonly used measure of each. Both are based on income, not expenditure (see Brewer et al, 2006b).

The measure of *inequality* we use is the Gini coefficient. This is a number between 0 and 1 (or 0% and 100%), where 0 represents complete equality – everybody has the same income – and 1 represents complete inequality – a single person receives all the income in the economy. See Brewer et al (2006c) for an explanation of how the Gini coefficient is calculated.

We define the rate of *poverty* as the proportion of people who live in households with incomes below 60% of the median. This is a widely used poverty line in the UK, and one that the government has adopted for assessing progress towards its child poverty targets. It is a measure of relative poverty, because whether someone is poor depends not only on their income but also on the incomes of the rest of society; measures of so-called absolute poverty, on the other hand, count how many people are below a certain fixed level, regardless of the incomes of the rest of society.

In both cases, incomes are measured at the household level, after state benefits have been added and taxes deducted, but without deducting housing costs, and are adjusted for household size using the McClements equivalence scale (see DWP, 2006a, for more details on the measure of income).

the poverty rate). The correlation of poverty and inequality with other points in the distribution of work incentives (10th, 25th, 75th and 90th centiles), not shown here, is almost as strong.

The policy trade-off between work incentives and redistribution is one possible driver of the correlation between incentives and poverty/inequality rates: at times, governments have implemented redistributive policies that have served both to reduce poverty and inequality and to weaken work incentives, while at other times they have been less redistributive, allowing poverty and inequality to rise but strengthening work incentives. However, to tell a simple historical story for Britain along these lines would be to read too much into the data. There are many other causal relationships that could affect the statistical connection seen here.

Most obviously, people may respond to increased work incentives and thereby increase their incomes. Such income increases would reduce absolute poverty, but their impact on the relative poverty and inequality measures considered here is ambiguous: it would depend on by how much poor people increased their incomes relative to rich people. As a further complication, there may be crucial lags between cause and effect: for example, an increased incentive to progress may lead people to invest in strengthening their skills, thereby increasing their income in the long term but maybe even reducing their income in the short term.

More importantly, factors other than tax and benefit policy affect both work incentives and poverty/inequality. Demographic changes such as an increase in the rate of family break-up are one such factor. Another is the state of the wider economy: changes to employment rates, earnings growth and so on have large effects on work incentives and the income distribution, and their implications for the measures considered here are not always obvious.

The importance of these other factors should not be underestimated. The strong correlations between work incentive measures and poverty/inequality measures mentioned above do not primarily reflect year-to-year fluctuations in the measures; rather, they reflect the fact that the broad long-term trend has been for work incentives to strengthen on average and for relative poverty and inequality to rise. Yet other work (cited in the following paragraph) suggests that these long-term trends are not caused solely, or even predominantly, by real tax and benefit changes.

It would be informative, therefore, to compare the changes in work incentives and the income distribution caused directly by tax and benefit changes alone. The changes in average work incentives since 1979 are decomposed into tax and benefit changes and various other factors in Adam et al (2006), summarised in Chapter 3 of this report. Decomposing changes in poverty and inequality is beyond the scope of this study, but has been done previously by Clark and Leicester (2004, figure 2) for inequality up to 2001 and by Dickens and Ellwood (2003, figure 8.4) for poverty up to 1999.[9]

As noted in Box 3.1, it is important to recognise that decompositions have limitations. At best, they capture only the direct effect of policy: they show what poverty, inequality and work incentives would have looked like in the absence of policy changes, *holding all other factors constant*. But in practice people may well have behaved differently if different policies had been in place, and so this decomposition approach cannot tell us, for example, how far tax and benefit changes reduced poverty by encouraging people to move into work. Answering that kind of question requires estimation of sophisticated behavioural models; this analysis illustrates only the direct effect of policies on work incentives and the income distribution.

With this caveat in mind, these three decompositions tell a story for the 1980s that is broadly consistent with the simple interpretation given above. Personal tax and benefit changes (just benefit changes, in the case of Dickens and Ellwood's study) in the early 1980s acted to reduce poverty and inequality and to weaken average work incentives. Policy changes in the mid-1980s were fairly neutral, while from around 1987 to 1990 they increased poverty and inequality and strengthened work incentives. The story is much less clear for the 1990s, however. Over the decade as a whole, policy changes acted both to reduce poverty and inequality and to strengthen work incentives, although the year-to-year fluctuations in the different measures are not closely aligned.

Overall, the cumulative effect of real tax and benefit changes from 1979 to 1999 appears to have been to reduce poverty and inequality *and* to strengthen average work incentives (see Table 4.1 in Box 4.2) – rather contrary to the impression one might take from the raw trends shown in Figures 4.1 to 4.3. According to these decompositions, in 1999 the mean replacement rate was 3.0 percentage points lower, the mean EMTR 3.4 percentage points lower, the poverty rate 3.7 percentage points lower, and the Gini coefficient 1.3 percentage points lower than they would have been if the policies implemented by the incoming 1979 Conservative government had remained in place. Box 4.2 also shows how these decompositions vary by family type.

This finding would seem to contradict the proposition that there is a policy trade-off between work incentives and redistribution. There are several possible explanations for this apparent contradiction. One is that it is an illusion caused by measurement difficulties:

---

9   The decomposition in Dickens and Ellwood (2003) is slightly different from our decomposition of work incentives, and their measure of poverty is slightly different from other studies: their study measures income at the family level and without deducting taxes, separates out just the effect of benefit changes, not tax changes, and does so using a regression of benefit receipt on family characteristics rather than full micro-simulation modelling.

- Dickens and Ellwood (2003) look only at benefit changes, not tax changes. It is possible that tax reforms acted to increase poverty rates, so that including them would yield a different result for the impact of reforms on poverty. In addition to this, their regression-based approach is not as accurate as the micro-simulation approach used by the other two studies, and they use a slightly different definition of income.
- Our decomposition of work incentives looks only at people in work. It is possible that tax and benefit reforms would have a different impact on incentives if the incentives faced by non-workers were considered (and non-workers are, of course, far more likely than workers to be in poverty).
- The type of decomposition pursued in these studies can give different results depending on the order of decomposition.
- There are many other possible measures of the distribution of income and work incentives; it is possible that these would reveal a different pattern. As well as alternative poverty lines or measures of average work incentives, there are also more nuanced outcomes, such as the depth of poverty or the distribution of work incentives away from the average, which might have been differently affected by policy reforms. A single summary measure rarely provides a complete picture.

A second possible factor in explaining how policy appears both to reduce poverty and inequality and strengthen work incentives is the overall generosity of the personal tax and benefit system. As noted in Chapter 1, increased spending can ease the overall trade-off between work incentives and redistribution. It is possible that the personal tax and benefit system was more generous in 1999 than in 1979, allowing both poverty and work incentive measures to look better. This extra generosity could be funded by higher borrowing, by reduced spending on public services, or by increases in company and

Box 4.2: Work incentives and poverty rates for different family types

This chapter examines the historical relationship between average work incentives and poverty and inequality in the population as a whole. But it is also possible to look at the relationship between poverty rates and work incentives within family types. Broadly speaking, the pattern seen across the population as a whole – that work incentives tend to be stronger in years when poverty rates are lower – is mirrored within each family type, but this correlation is weaker and less consistent than for the whole population. Most strikingly, the correlation is much weaker for parents than for adults in families without children.

One possible explanation for this is the large increases in state financial support for children that have been seen since 1979 (documented in Adam and Brewer, 2004). Increased spending can ease the overall trade-off between work incentives and redistribution, so increased support for parents may have helped to counteract the tendency seen in the population as a whole for poverty to rise when work incentives strengthened. The redistribution away from families without children that is implicit in this increased support for parents makes the trade-off correspondingly starker for those without children. However, as the rest of this chapter makes clear, there are many other factors that may be at work, and this can be only a tentative hypothesis.

Dickens and Ellwood (2003, table 8.1) try to isolate the direct effect of benefit reforms alone from 1979 to 1999 on the poverty rates of different family types in 1999. Table 4.1 compares this with a similar decomposition of average work incentives for different family types. The changes are rather dominated by lone parents, but it is hard to discern any clear relationship between how far policy changes strengthened average work incentives for a particular family type and how far they reduced that family type's poverty rate. As for the population as a whole, it is difficult to derive any firm conclusions about the trade-off between redistribution and incentives from this comparison.

Table 4.1: Effect of tax and benefit reforms between 1979 and 1999 on poverty, inequality and work incentives for different groups

	Percentage point change attributed to real policy reforms, 1979–99			
	Mean RR among workers	Mean EMTR among workers	Poverty rate	Inequality
Lone parents	−4.3	+5.8	−10.9	–
Fathers in couples	+1.6	+1.2	−2.3	–
Mothers in couples	+0.1	−6.0	−2.3	–
Single people without children	−1.8	−4.2	−6.5	–
Men in couples without children	−6.7	−4.9	−1.9	–
Women in couples without children	−2.7	−6.4	−1.9	–
All	−1.6	−3.2	−3.7	−1.3

Notes and sources: Column marked 'Poverty rate' from Dickens and Ellwood (2003), column marked 'Inequality' from Clark and Leicester (2004), other columns from authors' calculations. Excludes families containing any adults aged over 55, the self-employed, or adults receiving a disability benefit. Replacement rates (RRs) evaluated at 40 hours for all except for lone parents, where we use 20 hours.

indirect taxes: remember that all of this analysis ignores VAT, excise duties, employer national insurance contributions and corporation tax. Borrowing, public services and non-personal taxes affect the real incomes (or well-being more generally) and work incentives of current and future generations, so these should perhaps be thought of as complementary aspects of a broader incentives–redistribution trade-off we would like to measure.

Finally, the 'purest' explanation for tax and benefit reforms seeming both to reduce poverty and to strengthen work incentives is that governments may have moved towards a 'tagging' approach to redistribution. As explained in Chapter 1, this can genuinely alleviate the tension between work incentives and redistribution, albeit with other drawbacks.

It would be possible to explore each of these explanations in more depth: to look at UK policy on tagging and at the overall generosity of the personal tax and benefit system, and to redo the decompositions to try to reduce the measurement problems described above. However, we do not attempt to do so in this study. Rather, the lesson we draw from this chapter is that it is extremely difficult, if not impossible, to draw firm conclusions about the trade-off between redistribution and work incentives from looking at broad historical trends. There are simply too many complications and conflicting influences to try to separate out: behavioural responses to policy reforms, demographic and economic changes that happen alongside policy changes, measurement problems, and above all the fact that the policy trade-off itself is complicated, with several reforms happening at once, different groups being affected in different ways by a reform, and the overall generosity of the tax and benefit system changing. In the next chapter, we take a different approach: rather than trying to pick out patterns from a messy history, we simulate single reforms in an unchanging world and look in detail at the effects.

The effects of possible tax and benefit reforms on work incentives and the distribution of income

In this chapter we examine the effects of a variety of tax and benefit reforms on measures of financial work incentives and the income distribution. We examine nine ways in which the government might spend a given amount of money to try to reduce poverty and/or strengthen work incentives. For comparison, we also look at one way in which the government might raise that amount of money.

All reforms are applied to the April 2005 tax and benefit system and effects are estimated using TAXBEN run on data from the 2002–03 Family Resources Survey (FRS) uprated to 2005 prices. As in the analysis presented in Chapters 3 and 4, we exclude individuals in families in which someone is aged over 55 or self-employed (see Table 3.1), and we only look at the work incentives of those currently in work.

The revenue-raising reform we consider is a 0.5 percentage point increase in all rates of employee and self-employed national insurance contributions (NICs). This seems to be a reasonable baseline, since an increase in these rates was the last major tax-raising measure directly affecting the personal sector and a future increase has not been ruled out by the present government. Using TAXBEN, we estimate that this reform would raise £2.23 billion, assuming no behavioural response to the reform.

The nine revenue-reducing reforms we consider are as follows:

(1) Reducing all rates of employee and self-employed NICs by 0.5 percentage points.
(2) Increasing all adult allowances for non-pensioners in income support, income-based jobseeker's allowance, housing benefit and council tax benefit by 18.6%.
(3) Increasing child benefit rates (and child additions to housing benefit and council tax benefit) by £3.38 per week.
(4) Increasing the starting-rate limit in income tax by £732 per year.
(5) Cutting the housing benefit taper rate from 65% to 36.1%.
(6) Increasing each of the basic element and the couple and lone parent element of working tax credit (WTC) by £518 per year (leaving the income threshold for families receiving only child tax credit [CTC] unchanged).
(7) Increasing the child element of CTC (and child additions to housing benefit and council tax benefit) by £343 per year.
(8) Introducing a £1,955 per year premium in CTC, housing benefit and council tax benefit for families with three or more children (in CTC, this premium is tapered away like the existing family element).

(9)   Increasing the baby addition in CTC by £482 per year and extend it to families with a child under the age of five.

The first three of these are starkly contrasting archetypes: an across-the-board cut in tax on earnings, an increase in means-tested benefits for the poorest, and an increase in non-income-related benefits for a poorer-than-average group. The next three are subtler reforms, which affect the trade-off in interesting, less obvious ways. The final three focus particularly on reforms to CTC, the most obvious tool with which the government might seek to meet its challenging child poverty targets for 2010 and 2020.

The magnitude of each of these reforms has been chosen so that the cost (assuming no behavioural response) would be £2.23 billion, the same amount as would be raised by the NICs increase described above.[10] The scale of this reform is essentially arbitrary, and so the absolute magnitudes of our estimates are not particularly informative. Rather, the key features of our results are the *relative* magnitudes of the effects for different groups of people and for different reforms.

The importance of assuming no behavioural response in this chapter should be stressed. As discussed in Chapter 1, our aim is to illustrate how different reforms directly affect incomes and work incentives, not to predict how people would respond to the changes in incentives. However, in practice there would be some such responses. The overall progressiveness of the tax and benefit system means that, to the extent that a particular reform prompts people to work more, it is likely to increase their tax liabilities and reduce their benefit and tax credit entitlements, offsetting any direct cost of the reform. Thus the reforms listed above would not all cost/raise exactly the £2.23 billion we assume: those that strengthen work incentives will cost less, while those that weaken work incentives will cost more.[11] But since a particular reform might affect different people's work incentives in different ways, we do not attempt to judge the direction of the overall effect, let alone the size.

It should also be noted that we assume full take-up of benefits and tax credits throughout. This might lead us to overestimate the exchequer cost, and the corresponding gains to families, associated with increases in benefits and tax credits, since not all families would take up their additional entitlements. On the other hand, such increases in entitlements might induce some families who do not currently take up their entitlements to do so, thus leading us to underestimate the exchequer cost and corresponding gains to families. The effect of ignoring non-take-up on work incentive measures is somewhat more complicated but also ambiguous. The direction and size of any bias in our analysis is therefore unclear.

Table 5.1 shows, both overall and for the six different family types analysed in Chapter 3, how the various reforms affect the average and quartile points of replacement rates at 40 hours, and what proportions of the population see their rates rise and fall. Table 5.2

---

[10]   Where possible, we compared these TAXBEN costings with those implied by the *Tax Ready Reckoner* (HM Treasury, 2005 and previous years). We found no alarming discrepancies between the two.

[11]   At the extreme, it is possible that the behavioural response to a give-away could be so large that the cost would be zero or even negative. This could happen if, for example, tax rates are above the revenue-maximising level (the 'Laffer bound'), in which case cutting them would increase people's incomes, strengthen work incentives *and* raise revenue for the government: a genuine win–win situation. Again, we make no comment here on the likelihood of such a situation arising. The reforms also create incentives to change behaviour other than work, which might also have an important impact on the costs of the policies. Such behaviour ranges from tax avoidance activity to childbearing decisions. One important example, benefit and tax credit take-up decisions, is discussed in the next paragraph.

presents similar statistics for effective marginal tax rates (EMTRs) among the working population, while Tables 5.3 and 5.4 show what this means for the proportion of working individuals facing EMTRs in particular ranges. Table 5.5 shows the gain or loss experienced by each tenth of the income distribution as a proportion of income; Figures 5.1 to 5.4 illustrate these distributional effects in cash terms, using the same vertical scale for each reform. These tables and figures are collected at the end of the chapter for ease of reference.

As with our measures of poverty and inequality in the previous chapter, we use families' current income to analyse the distributional impact of reforms. This choice is not as innocuous as it might seem. Current income is a limited measure of material living standards, let alone well-being more broadly conceived. In particular, current income is an imperfect guide to (expected) lifetime income: for many of those recorded in household surveys as having low income and referred to in this report as 'poor', low income is a temporary phenomenon – for example, the survey might be conducted with a respondent who is between jobs, or with a usually high-earning person who is taking a break from the labour market to raise children, or with a young graduate who has started work on low pay but can expect rapid progression in future years.[12] Measures that redistribute from high (current) income households to low (current) income households will therefore be less successful than this suggests in redistributing income from lifetime-rich to lifetime-poor. Taxes and benefits redistribute income over the life-cycle as well as between households: thus the same people may be net recipients from the state when they are early in their career progression and facing the costs of raising children, but then pay it back in higher taxes when they are at the height of their earning power and the children have left home, before receiving a substantial transfer from the state when they retire. Thus, for example, the final reform we consider, which redistributes to households containing young children, will largely be redirecting income to a particular period in people's lives, whereas the penultimate reform, which targets households containing many children, will do more to redistribute to people who have low income and high costs over their life as a whole: this distinction will not be reflected in the simple distributional analysis shown here.

Below, we examine each of the reforms in turn. At the end of the chapter we compare the various reforms and draw conclusions.

Increasing NIC rates

The revenue-raising reform we consider is a 0.5 percentage point increase in all rates of employee and self-employed NICs.

The effect of this on individuals' EMTRs is fairly straightforward: 90.5% of workers see their EMTR rise, in most cases by 0.5%. This happens to cause a large shift – some 4% of workers, or around 720,000 individuals – from the group facing EMTRs of 60.1–70% in Table 5.3 to the group facing 70.1–80%, essentially because a large cluster of individuals facing an EMTR of exactly 70% before the reform (made up of 22% basic-rate income tax, 11% contracted-in NICs and 37% CTC/WTC taper) faces 70.5% after the reform and is therefore in a different range.

For single people (with and without children), the effect on replacement rates at 40 hours is also simple: in-work income falls while out-of-work income is unaffected, so the

---

[12] Current expenditure might be better than current income as a measure of living standards, since people can smooth their expenditure by saving and borrowing at particular times according to whether they expect their average income over their lifetime to be higher or lower than their current income: see Brewer et al (2006b).

replacement rate rises for over 96% of these individuals (Table 5.1). The effect for individuals in couples is more nuanced. Those with non-working partners see their replacement rates rise much as for single people. But those with working partners see their out-of-work income fall as well as their in-work income (since their partner's earnings are being taxed more heavily), so their replacement rate may rise or fall depending on both partners' earnings. Thus, among women in childless couples – many of whom have relatively high-earning partners – more see their replacement rate fall (50.5%) than rise (31.9%). Overall, three quarters of individuals see their replacement rate at 40 hours rise while 15% see it fall; the mean, median, 25th centile and 75th centile all rise by 0.1 percentage point.

Turning now to the distributional impact, 0.5% of earnings (above the earnings threshold) obviously comes to more in cash terms for higher earners, and Figure 5.1 correspondingly shows larger cash losses for successively higher-income decile groups of families, rising from less than a penny per week on average for the poorest tenth to £5.80 per week for the richest tenth. Slightly less obvious is the impact in percentage terms. In fact, losses as a proportion of income are also larger for successively higher decile groups, as Table 5.5 shows. One reason for this is that the NIC rise applies only above the £94 per week earnings threshold, and so the proportion of *total* earnings taken in extra NICs is higher for higher earners – indeed, many towards the bottom of the income distribution do not have any earnings at all above the £94 threshold, including those who do not work at all. A second reason is that, because of the progressive tax and benefit system, a given proportion of a family's gross earnings corresponds to a larger proportion of net family income towards the top of the income distribution.

To summarise, then, this reform takes more from higher-income families than from lower-income families; it increases the EMTRs faced by most workers; and it increases the replacement rates at 40 hours faced by most people, although many individuals with relatively high-earning partners see their replacement rates fall.

Reducing NIC rates

The first revenue-reducing reform we consider, a 0.5 percentage point cut in all rates of employee and self-employed NICs, is almost a mirror image of the 0.5 percentage point rise examined above, and we do not, therefore, discuss it in any detail. Suffice it to say that this reform gives more to higher-income families than to lower-income families, both in cash terms and as a percentage of income; it reduces the EMTRs faced by most workers, typically by 0.5 percentage points; and it increases the replacement rates at 40 hours faced by most people, although many individuals with relatively high-earning partners see their replacement rates fall. More details can be gathered from Tables 5.1 to 5.5 and Figure 5.2, and inferred from the discussion above.

Increasing income support and other safety-net benefits

The second revenue-reducing reform we consider is an 18.6% increase in all adult allowances for non-pensioners in income support, income-based jobseeker's allowance, housing benefit and council tax benefit. This takes the allowance from £56.20 per week to £66.65 per week for a single person (aged 25 or over) and from £88.15 to £104.55 for a couple (both aged 18 or over).

A straightforward increase of this kind in the main safety-net benefits is extremely progressive: the first (poorest) income decile group gains by £7.57 per week on average, or 9.4% of income, while the top end of the income distribution is virtually unaffected, as shown in Table 5.5 and Figure 5.2.

It also greatly damages the incentive to work. Over half the population see their replacement rate at 40 hours rise, the remainder largely comprising people with working partners whose family income would be too high for safety-net benefits whether or not they worked. The mean replacement rate rises by 1.9 percentage points, while the median rises by 1.2 percentage points – far bigger rises than for any other reform we consider. One mitigating factor is that, with the exception of lone parents, the biggest rises in replacement rates are experienced by groups with relatively low replacement rates to start with: the median rate for single people without children rises 4.2 percentage points from a base of 27.1%, whereas that for mothers in couples rises only 0.3 percentage points from a base of 67.8%. Thus overall the 75th centile of replacement rates rises by less (1.4 percentage points from a base of 64.9%) than the 25th centile (3.1 percentage points from a base of 30.8%), although this is not generally true *within* family types.

The effect on workers' EMTRs is more concentrated: a relatively small number of individuals in low-income families face massively increased EMTRs. The proportion of workers facing EMTRs above 70% increases by 0.6 percentage points (around 100,000 people), and the proportion facing EMTRs over 90% rises by 0.3 percentage points (around 58,000 people). Thus the mean EMTR increases by 0.3 percentage points, but this is a result of increases experienced by only 1.6% of workers. Only among lone parents is an effect visible over a substantial part of the distribution. It is notable that the worst incentive effects from this reform, taking EMTRs and replacement rates together, are on lone parents – the poorest group and the group with the worst average incentives to start with, as discussed in Chapter 3.

This reform is a classic example of one extreme of the work incentive– redistribution trade-off. The money is extremely well targeted at the poorest families, but the cost is a large reduction in the incentive to work at all for most people without working partners.

Increasing child benefit

The next reform we consider is increasing child benefit rates by £3.38 per week, from £17 to £20.38 for the first child and from £11.40 to £14.78 for subsequent children. We also consider increasing child additions to housing benefit and council tax benefit by the same amount to ensure that families receiving these benefits gain from the change to child benefit in full.

Increasing a universal, non-taxable benefit has a negligible effect on EMTRs. It does affect replacement rates, however. Since increasing child benefit raises parents' in-work and out-of-work incomes by the same cash amount, it increases almost all parents' replacement rates somewhat: by an average (mean) of 0.5 percentage points for lone parents, 0.4 percentage points for fathers in couples and 0.3 percentage points for mothers in couples; childless people are, of course, unaffected. Note, however, that this kind of equal increase in in-work and out-of-work income would have no effect on participation tax rates, our alternative measure of the incentive to work at all.

The policy has a modest redistributive effect (see Table 5.5 and Figure 5.2). Families all gain the same amount in cash terms per child, £3.38. But children are not evenly distributed across the income distribution. They are most under-represented in the poorest decile group, which gains only £0.55 per week on average; but they are very much over-represented in the second decile group (which gains £3.76 per week on average, implying more than one child per family in this group), with successively fewer children in higher decile groups, so that the richest decile group gains £1.06 per week on average. The fall in gains from the second to the 10th decile group is more pronounced as a proportion of income, declining from 1.9% of income for the second decile group to 0.1% for the 10th (Table 5.5); at 0.7% of income, the poorest decile group's gain is around the middle of the range on this measure.

Increasing child benefit is a classic example of 'tagging' using a categorical benefit (discussed in Chapter 1). Child benefit is not explicitly means-tested, so it does not increase EMTRs; but since the number of children in the family is negatively correlated with income, the benefits accrue disproportionately to the poor. The policy achieves only modest redistribution, but with relatively benign effects on financial work incentives (replacement rates rise slightly, but participation tax rates and EMTRs are unaffected). Clearly the use of other 'tags' that are more closely correlated with income would have a greater distributional impact with similarly little damage to work incentives. Potential disadvantages of this approach are discussed briefly in Chapter 1.

Increasing the starting-rate limit

The introduction of a 10% starting rate of income tax, replacing the 20% lower rate introduced by the Conservatives (which had applied over a wider range of income), was a flagship policy of the New Labour government's first term in 1997. The government clearly viewed this as a good way to strengthen work incentives: it was announced as a policy 'to make work pay' and 'to put work first in the tax and benefit system'; but it was also claimed that 'those on the lowest incomes … will gain more [than basic- and higher-rate taxpayers], because the three rate structure helps to target the gains from the 10p rate on the lowest paid' (Budget 1999). Labour's 2001 general election manifesto pledged to 'extend the 10p tax band'. In the event, the 10% band was not extended (beyond statutory indexation) in Labour's second term, and the pledge was not repeated in its 2005 manifesto. It seems an interesting policy to consider because of this history, because the government has claimed this as a policy that both strengthens work incentives and helps the poor most, and because cuts in income tax are often the first port of call in public discussions of how to strengthen work incentives.

The policy we consider is a £732-per-year increase in the starting-rate limit, widening the starting-rate band at the expense of the basic-rate band (and leaving untouched the point at which higher-rate tax starts to be paid). This increases the starting-rate limit from £2,090 to £2,822; for most taxpayers (with a tax-free personal allowance of £4,895), the income level at which basic-rate tax starts to be due therefore rises from £6,985 to £7,717.

This has the effect of reducing the marginal income tax rate from 22% to 10% for individuals with incomes in this £732 range; individuals with higher incomes see no change in their marginal income tax rate, but their income tax bills all fall by £87.84 per year (12% of £732), and this increase in after-tax income moves some people off benefits, thereby reducing their EMTRs. Each of these factors has a big effect on marginal rates, but only for a small number of workers, so only 3% see their EMTRs fall. The mean EMTR falls by 0.2 percentage points, with the biggest average falls experienced by working mothers in couples. There is a substantial shift in the distribution of EMTRs from those facing 30–40% EMTRs to those facing 20–30%, and a smaller shift from those facing 60–70% to those facing 50–60%.

A substantial proportion of people with working partners see their replacement rate at 40 hours rise, because the increase in their out-of-work family income (via the partner's lower tax bill) is proportionally larger than the increase in their in-work family income (via both partners' lower tax bills). This is a similar effect observed above for the NIC reforms, although the people whose replacement rates rise are different in this case because the gains from the policy do not rise with earnings as much. Unlike with the NIC reforms, some people without working partners also see their replacement rate fall: this is because income tax, unlike NICs, is payable on income other than earnings (primarily some types of investment and state benefit income), and so the reform increases some people's out-of-work income as well as their in-work income. These groups with rising replacement rates are very much in a minority, however: 13.6% of individuals see their replacement rate at 40 hours rise, while 79.1% see it fall; the mean and median replacement rates both fall by 0.1 percentage points. The biggest average falls are experienced by lone parents, followed by single people without children.

The maximum reduction in income tax from this policy – £87.84 per year – goes to any individual with an annual income above £7,717, while individuals with incomes below £6,985 gain nothing at all. The cash gains are therefore greater for successively richer decile groups (Figure 5.3), because richer decile groups contain more workers and because those workers have higher average earnings. The poorest decile group is barely affected at all. In proportional terms (Table 5.5), the largest gains are towards the middle of the income distribution, at around 0.5% of income.

Widening the starting-rate band is not, then, a strong way to increase the incomes of the poor: most of them currently pay less than basic-rate income tax and so do not benefit at all, while the largest cash gains accrue to those above the new starting-rate limit. The effect on financial work incentives is positive, but not dramatic: EMTRs fall substantially but only for a small number of people; replacement rates at 40 hours fall for most people, but rise for a substantial minority.

Reducing the housing benefit taper

Housing benefit is currently withdrawn at a rate of 65p per £1 of after-tax income. That is one of the main reasons for people facing extremely high EMTRs, especially when housing benefit recipients are also paying income tax and NICs and/or facing withdrawal of tax credits or council tax benefit. Here we explore reducing this withdrawal rate to 36.1p per £1.[13] This is similar in spirit to the reduction in the taper rate for in-work support that the government implemented when replacing family credit by working families' tax credit in 1999.

Reducing the housing benefit taper rate does reduce the number of people facing very high EMTRs: the proportion of workers facing EMTRs above 60% falls from 11.1% to 9.9%, a reduction of around 225,000 people. Being on the housing benefit taper, these families that face strengthened incentives to progress are also towards the bottom of the income distribution. However, the downside is that many more people are floated onto housing benefit (albeit with the new lower taper rate), so that the proportion of workers facing EMTRs of between 50% and 60% rises by a hefty 2.8 percentage points (almost half

---

[13] Because housing benefit is assessed on income after income tax and NICs have been deducted and after tax credits have been added, the reduction in the housing benefit taper rate from 65% to 36.1% does not mean that recipients' EMTRs fall by 28.9 percentage points. For someone paying basic-rate income tax and standard-rate NICs and on a tax credit taper, an extra £1 of earnings means only 30p extra income for the housing benefit assessment (since 22p is lost in extra income tax, 11p in extra NICs, and 37p in reduced tax credits). It is this remaining 30p that is reduced by 36.1% rather than 65% as a result of the reform, so the reduction in the overall EMTR is 0.289 x 0.3, that is, 8.7 percentage points. The EMTR for this person falls from 89.5% to 80.8%, or from 95.5% to 86.8% if they are also on a council tax benefit taper.

a million people) – a combination of people newly entitled to housing benefit and existing housing benefit recipients still facing moderately high marginal rates. In all, 3.6% of workers see their EMTR rise while 2.6% see it fall; both groups, but especially the latter, are disproportionately made up of lone parents. The mean EMTR rises by 0.2 percentage points, while the median is unchanged.

Replacement rates at 40 hours rise for 7.1% of individuals and fall for 8.3%; again, both groups, but especially the latter, are disproportionately made up of lone parents. The mean replacement rate falls by 0.2 percentage points, while the median rises by 0.2 percentage points. The reasons for these mixed effects on replacement rates are complicated. Anyone who is already on the housing benefit taper, or who is brought onto the taper by the reduction in the withdrawal rate, sees their in-work income rise. For workers whose earnings are the only source of family income, this rise in in-work income means a fall in their replacement rate, since their out-of-work income is unchanged (they receive full housing benefit with or without the reform). But for people whose other sources of family income (such as savings income, other benefits and tax credits, or a partner's earnings) would put them on the (post-reform) housing benefit taper even if they were out of work, out-of-work income rises; thus, with rises in both in-work and out-of-work income, the effect on these people's replacement rates is ambiguous. And replacement rates unambiguously rise for people whose out-of-work income is increased by the reform but whose earnings make them too rich to get housing benefit even after the reform.

As a proportion of income, the gains from reducing the housing benefit taper rate are broadly progressively distributed, with the largest gain (1.5% of income) accruing to the second decile group and the smallest (0.1% of income) to the top decile group, although the gains for the poorest decile group (0.4% of income) are not particularly large (Table 5.5). In cash terms (Figure 5.3), a relationship between income decile group and average gain can only faintly be discerned.

Cutting the housing benefit taper rate, then, is weakly redistributive, providing the largest gains to the second, third and fourth decile groups but doing little for the poorest tenth. Its effect on replacement rates is complicated and ambiguous. EMTRs rise on average, with more people facing fairly high rates of 50-60%, but the number of (mostly poor) people facing even higher EMTRs than this is considerably reduced.

Increasing WTC

The next reform we consider is an increase in the WTC. We increase each of the basic element and the couple and lone parent element of WTC by £518 per year, taking the basic element from £1,620 to £2,138 and the extra received by lone parents and couples from £1,595 to £2,113. This naturally means that the income level at which WTC runs out, and at which CTC starts being withdrawn from families eligible for that too, rises; however, we leave unchanged the income threshold at which CTC starts to be withdrawn for families not entitled to WTC, so that only families eligible for WTC are affected by the reform.

The full gains from this reform accrue to those who are currently receiving WTC, or to parents who have too much income to be on WTC but little enough to receive CTC (beyond the family element). Working families with incomes slightly above the end of this tax credit taper (within £1,400 for single people without children, £2,800 for lone parents and couples) are floated onto tax credits and gain by a lesser amount. Families with higher incomes than this, and families who do not meet the work conditions in WTC, are unaffected. The reform therefore benefits low-income families, but the work requirement means that many of the poorest are unaffected. Table 5.5 and Figure 5.3 show that the gains peak in the third decile group, which gains by £7.39 per week on average, or 2.9% of income.

Given that the gains are restricted to working families, it is perhaps surprising that the effect of this reform on replacement rates at 40 hours is not particularly strong: the mean replacement rate is broadly unaffected and the median actually rises by 0.6 percentage points, although the 25th and 75th centile both fall (by 0.2 and 0.1 percentage points respectively); more people see their replacement rate rise (20.1%) than fall (18.7%). The key to this is again people with working partners. Replacement rates fall for 92.7% of lone parents and 14% of single people without children (with the mean falling by 3.0 and 0.3 percentage points respectively); no one in either of these groups sees their replacement rate rise, since their in-work income may be increased and their out-of-work income is unaffected. The pattern is similar for people with non-working partners. But many people with working partners see their replacement rate rise, in particular where the family would benefit from the reform with only one partner working but where the additional income from a second earner would reduce or eliminate their tax credit entitlement, or even where it would leave it unchanged. For the potential second earner in these cases, in-work income rises (if at all) by no more than out-of-work income, and his or her replacement rate rises.[14]

The effect on EMTRs is also ambiguous. Some people become newly entitled to tax credits, and face a higher EMTR as a result of being on the tax credit taper. But for other people, the increased income from tax credits moves them off the end of the housing benefit or council tax benefit taper, reducing their EMTR. The latter group is slightly poorer on average, and is disproportionately made up of lone parents: this is the only group in which more workers see their EMTR fall than rise (12.5% versus 5.3%) and in which the mean EMTR falls (by 1.8 percentage points; the median is unaffected). Among workers as a whole, the mean EMTR rises by 1.0 percentage point while the median is unchanged; 4.4% see their EMTR rise, and 1.3% see it fall. The two offsetting effects on EMTRs can be seen in Tables 5.2 and 5.3: there is a large shift in the distribution of EMTRs from the 30–40% group to the 60–70% group: in particular, many people move from facing just basic-rate income tax and standard NICs (33% in total if contracted into the state second pension, 31.6% if contracted out[15]) to facing basic-rate income tax, standard NICs and the tax credit taper (70% in total if contracted in, 68.6% if contracted out). But at the same time, many of the people floated off the end of the housing benefit or council tax benefit taper were previously facing extremely high EMTRs, so there is a reduction of around one fifth (0.6% of all workers) in the number of workers facing EMTRs above 70%.

Overall, then, the effects of increasing WTC are interestingly mixed. It helps workers on low incomes, but not the poorest, who tend to be out of work; it increases EMTRs on

---

[14] Some individuals with working partners might see their replacement rate fall, however, for a variety of reasons. For example, having a second worker might give the family entitlement to tax credits (higher after the reform) by satisfying the work conditions for basic WTC entitlement or for entitlement to childcare support, in which case in-work income rises while out-of-work income is unaffected. Or, in addition to tax credits, a family might be entitled to housing benefit or council tax benefit if only the first partner works, but not if the second partner also works. Then the increased tax credit entitlement is offset by reduced housing benefit/council tax benefit entitlement in the one-earner case, so that the family's overall net income may rise by more if the second partner is in work than if the second partner is out of work, and the effect on the second partner's replacement rate is ambiguous.

[15] Again, we ignore the additional age-related NIC rebate that applies to people who are contracted out into defined contribution pension schemes.

average, but reduces them for a substantial (and low-income) minority, particularly lone parents; and it has mixed effects on replacement rates, which fall for many people without working partners (again, particularly lone parents) but rise for many people with working partners.

Increasing the child element of CTC

We next consider increasing the child element of CTC by £343 per year, from £1,690 to £2,033 per child. As with the child benefit increase considered above, we also consider increasing child additions to housing benefit and council tax benefit by the same amount, so that recipients of these benefits do not gain less from the reform. This is a politically interesting reform, since the child element of CTC (and its predecessors) is a tool the government has used in the past to help meet its child poverty targets – a challenge that remains for the coming years.

Increasing the child element of CTC is indeed highly progressive, as shown in Table 5.5 and Figure 5.4: with the exception of the poorest decile group (in which children are under-represented, as mentioned above), successively higher-income decile groups gain less from the reform, with the second decile group gaining £7.33 per week on average (or 3.7% of income) and the 10th decile group barely affected.

However, the effect on parents' work incentives is correspondingly weak (people without children are, of course, entirely unaffected by the reform). The mean replacement rate at 40 hours and the mean EMTR among workers both rise by 0.4 percentage points. A total of 30.6% of all workers see their replacement rate rise: this represents almost all lone parents, the vast majority of fathers in couples and about half of mothers in couples (parents whose replacement rates do not rise are those with relatively high-earning partners, with too much income to get the child element of CTC even out of work). Only 1.6% of workers see their EMTR rise (2.8% of lone parents, 4.7% of fathers in couples and 3.6% of mothers in couples), but those people mostly face very large rises, in the majority of cases taking their EMTR above 60%. Almost no one sees a fall in either measure of work incentives.

This is a classic increase in means-tested support: very successful in targeting money at the poor, but very weak for work incentives.

Introducing a big-family premium in CTC

The next reform we consider is the introduction of a new £1,955 per year premium in CTC for families with three or more children. We treat this as an addition to the existing family element of CTC, so that it is only tapered away above the second (£50,000) income threshold. As before, we introduce corresponding premiums in housing benefit and council tax benefit so that the gains are not reduced for recipients of these benefits.

Targeting the give-away entirely at the small group of families with three or more children means that the gains for this group are very large indeed: the vast majority of these families receive the full £1,955 per year, or £37.60 per week. The overall effect of this across the income distribution (Table 5.5 and Figure 5.4) resembles that of increasing the child element of CTC – the gain is highest for the second decile group (£5.96 per week on average, or 3.0% of income) and declines for higher decile groups – but is slightly less progressive.

EMTRs among workers are barely affected: they rise for only 0.6% of workers, with the mean and median virtually unchanged. The effect on replacement rates is worse: almost everyone with three or more children (7% of all individuals, representing 15.9% of lone parents, 17.6% of fathers in couples and 17.2% of mothers in couples) sees their replacement rate at 40 hours rise, since their in-work income rises by the same amount as (or occasionally less than) their out-of-work income; this increases the overall mean and median replacement rates by 0.1%. But note that our alternative measure of the incentive to work at all – participation tax rates – would be unchanged for those people with equal increases in in-work and out-of-work income.

This policy represents an interesting approach to reducing child poverty. It is less akin to the aggressive means-testing involved in increasing the child element of the CTC than to the non-means-tested 'tagging' approach embodied in a child benefit increase. The fact that it is withdrawn at incomes above £50,000 is barely relevant, since only a small minority of families with three or more children have incomes above this level.[16] For poverty reduction, it instead relies on restricting the gains to families with three or more children. Such large families are in fact much more likely to be in poverty than other families (see Adelman et al, 2003; Bradshaw et al, 2006), and this makes a big-family premium highly effective at helping the poor – much more so than a general increase in child benefit, and almost as much as an increase in the child element of CTC. At the same time, while the impact on work incentives is not quite as benign as for child benefit, it is much less detrimental than the child element of CTC.

Extending the baby addition in CTC

Finally, we consider increasing the baby addition in CTC by £482 per year (from £545 to £1,027) and extending it to families with a child under the age of five, rather than under the age of one as at present. This is in a similar spirit to the previous reform: it uses the fact that the presence of young children is a strong indicator of poverty, and the additional money is only withdrawn at the same high income levels. However, it is perhaps more in keeping with the government's previous reforms: Labour introduced the baby addition (in what was then children's tax credit) in April 2002, and also gradually removed the system of higher payments for older children in means-tested benefits, which had previously existed.

Under the McClements scale that we are using to produce equivalised income, having young children is less closely correlated with low income than having many children, and so the distributional impact is less progressive, with significant gains spreading right up to the ninth decile group (Table 5.5 and Figure 5.4). In addition, as discussed above, the redistribution entailed by this reform is rather more about redistribution over the life-cycle than redistribution between fundamentally different types of household (although clearly those who have more children over their lifetime gain more, and those who never have children or whose incomes are very high while their children are young do not gain at all).

Extending the baby addition in CTC also has a worse effect on replacement rates than introducing a big-family premium: 15.1% of individuals (33.4% of lone parents, 38.0% of fathers in couples and 37.6% of mothers in couples) see their replacement rate at 40 hours rise (although a few see it fall), with the mean and median both rising by 0.2 percentage points. The effect on EMTRs is still very small, however.

---

[16] In fact, since the family element of CTC must be withdrawn above £50,000 in any case, the relevant income level here is the end-point of the existing taper, £57,763 (or £65,917 for families with a child under one year old), thus capturing even fewer families.

To summarise, then, this policy achieves some redistribution, but not as much as the use of aggressive means-testing or simply better 'tags'. It leads to a modest increase in replacement rates, but has very little effect on EMTRs.

Comparing the reforms

The wide variety of reforms considered here gives rise to a correspondingly broad range of effects on financial work incentives and the income distribution. These are summarised in Table 5.6. Unsurprisingly, none of the reforms achieves both substantial redistribution of income to the poor and a substantial strengthening of average work incentives. The best way to spend a given amount of money depends on the government's priorities.

If the main concern is direct help for the poorest, then aggressively means-tested support is best: increasing income support (and the other safety-net benefits) and increasing the child element of CTC are the most progressive of the options considered here. Using the presence of three or more children as an indicator of poverty is also very progressive; using less strong indicators of poverty (increasing child benefit or extending the baby addition in CTC), increasing WTC, and reducing the housing benefit taper rate are only moderately progressive. Few would be surprised to learn that cutting NIC rates is regressive – the only reform considered that would benefit the rich most. What is perhaps less widely recognised is how little widening the 10% income tax band would do to help the poor compared with, say, increasing child benefit, let alone the more progressive reforms considered here. Increasing the main safety-net benefits is the only one of all these reforms, however, to yield sizeable gains for the poorest tenth: this group gains little from the other reforms since it contains few children, few people in work, and few people with high-enough incomes to pay basic rate income tax or receive much less than full housing benefit.

Tax cuts are the only reforms we consider that reduce the mean EMTR among workers: a fall of 0.5 percentage points from cutting NICs, and of 0.2 percentage points from increasing the starting-rate limit in income tax. Cutting NICs is the only reform for which falls in the EMTR are widespread, with 90.5% of workers seeing falls; the next highest figure is only 3%, for increasing the starting-rate limit (although the falls for those who do experience them are much larger than the falls from cutting NICs). These tax cuts also reduce average replacement rates; but in both cases this is complicated by the fact that many people with working partners see their out-of-work income rise and may therefore face higher replacement rates. This effect is also observed for the increase in WTC, and as a recurrent feature is worth highlighting: reforms that aim to encourage work by providing support exclusively or primarily to families with someone in work (that is, by cutting income taxes or increasing in-work benefits) may increase the incentive for someone in the family to be in work, but often reduce the incentive for a potential second earner to be in work.

Predictably, the reforms that do the most damage to work incentives are the same aggressively means-tested ones that do most to help the poor: increasing the main safety-net benefits and increasing the child element of CTC. In both cases, the incentive to work at all is substantially reduced for large numbers of people, and the incentive to progress once in work is massively reduced for relatively small numbers of low-income people. It is particularly notable that these are the reforms that do most to damage the work incentives (both replacement rates and EMTRs) of lone parents – the group facing the worst average incentives to start with. Taking all groups together, increasing WTC does even more damage to workers' average EMTRs, but its impact on replacement rates is more ambiguous. Increasing WTC is actually the reform that does most to strengthen the average (mean) EMTR and average replacement rate among lone parents. However, it has strongly detrimental effects on the average EMTR for workers in all other demographic groups, and detrimental effects on the average full-time replacement rate for all other groups except childless single people.

The reform that is most effective at reducing the number of people facing extremely high EMTRs is reducing the housing benefit taper rate: this reduces the number of workers facing EMTRs above 60% by about one ninth and reduces the number facing EMTRs above 80% by more than a quarter. Furthermore, those experiencing these falls in incentives to progress are almost all towards the bottom of the income distribution. But this comes at the cost of an even larger increase in the number of workers facing EMTRs of between 50% and 60%. Policy makers must thus strike a delicate balance between a relatively small number of people facing extremely weak incentives to progress and a much larger number facing quite weak incentives to progress.

The three reforms that (broadly speaking) adopt a tagging approach – increasing child benefit, introducing a big-family premium in CTC, and extending the baby addition in CTC – are fairly neutral with respect to work incentives. Increasing child benefit has a negligible effect on incentives to progress; it slightly reduces the incentive to work at all as measured by replacement rates, although not as measured by participation tax rates. The other two reforms are not quite as neutral, since they do involve an element of means-testing, but their effects on both incentives to progress and incentives to work at all remain slight. Given that these three reforms are also fairly progressive, they appear to represent quite attractive packages of income redistribution with minimal damage to work incentives. However, as mentioned in Chapter 1, the tagging approach also has its drawbacks. One problem is that it leaves behind those without the relevant 'tag' who are nevertheless poor, which is both a limitation in alleviating poverty and arguably unfair in itself: in particular, some complain that the present government's reforms have focused too much on child poverty and left behind the childless poor, a problem that all three of these reforms would exacerbate. A different kind of problem is the perverse incentives that tagging may create: this is most obvious for the big-family premium in CTC, which would introduce a £1,955-per-year (for 16–18 years) incentive for families to have a third child, over and above the incentives already provided by child benefit and other child-contingent support.[17]

All the nine give-aways we analyse in this chapter entail a cost to the exchequer of £2.23 billion (ignoring any behavioural response). But as noted in Chapter 1, increasing net government spending in this way can make the trade-off between work incentives and redistribution seem less severe than it really is. At least in the long run, financing such spending means taking money off people – presumably, therefore, making the poor worse off and/or weakening work incentives. So while we have examined each give-away in isolation in order to bring out its characteristics as clearly as possible, it might be fairer to think about them in combination with a reform that raises the same amount: hence our examination of an NIC increase at the beginning of the chapter. Note that, for a variety of reasons, the numbers reported here cannot simply be added together; nevertheless, when evaluating the give-aways it is worthwhile considering not simply their desirability per se but whether they are worth the income losses and weakening of incentives associated with the NIC rise. Of course, in practice there are as many and as varied ways of raising revenue as of distributing it, each with its own effects on work incentives and the income distribution.

---

[17] See Adam and Brewer (2004) for a quantification.

Table 5.1: Effects of the reforms on workers' replacement rates at 40 hours

	Full-time RR before reform (%)	Change in full-time replacement rate (percentage points)									
		NI up	NI down	IS up	CB up	SRL up	HB taper down	WTC up	CTC child up	CTC big family	CTC young
Single people without children											
Mean	32.0	+0.1	-0.1	+3.5	+0.0	-0.2	-0.5	-0.3	+0.0	+0.0	+0.0
Median	27.1	+0.1	-0.1	+4.2	+0.0	-0.2	+0.0	-0.0	+0.0	+0.0	+0.0
25th centile	20.3	+0.1	-0.1	+3.3	+0.0	-0.1	-0.0	+0.0	+0.0	+0.0	+0.0
75th centile	40.6	-0.0	-0.2	+3.9	+0.0	-0.2	+0.3	-0.3	+0.0	+0.0	+0.0
Proportion whose rate rises (%)		96.5	0.0	89.5	0.0	2.1	3.1	0.0	0.0	0.0	0.0
Proportion whose rate falls (%)		0.0	96.4	0.1	0.0	92.3	8.9	14.0	0.0	0.0	0.0
Lone parents											
Mean	62.3	+0.1	-0.1	+2.6	+0.5	-0.3	-1.6	-3.0	+1.1	+0.3	+0.6
Median	64.6	+0.2	-0.1	+3.0	+0.5	-0.3	-1.0	-3.8	+1.0	+0.3	+0.7
25th centile	52.3	+0.1	-0.1	+2.5	+0.7	-0.2	+0.5	-2.4	+1.3	+0.1	+0.5
75th centile	73.2	+0.2	-0.1	+3.1	+0.5	-0.3	-3.4	-4.1	+1.0	+0.6	+0.5
Proportion whose rate rises (%)		96.2	0.0	93.7	99.9	1.7	18.7	0.0	99.8	15.9	33.4
Proportion whose rate falls (%)		0.0	96.1	0.1	0.1	94.0	42.9	92.7	0.1	0.1	1.6
Men in childless couples											
Mean	44.8	+0.1	-0.1	+0.8	+0.0	-0.0	+0.2	+0.7	+0.0	+0.0	+0.0
Median	45.0	+0.1	-0.1	+0.7	+0.0	-0.0	+0.3	+1.3	+0.0	+0.0	+0.0
25th centile	35.4	+0.1	-0.0	+0.8	+0.0	+0.0	+0.2	+0.6	+0.0	+0.0	+0.0
75th centile	54.1	+0.0	-0.0	+0.6	+0.0	-0.1	+0.6	+1.3	+0.0	+0.0	+0.0
Proportion whose rate rises (%)		67.4	15.4	31.7	0.0	42.8	7.9	25.6	0.0	0.0	0.0
Proportion whose rate falls (%)		15.4	67.1	0.2	0.0	46.3	2.3	6.9	0.0	0.0	0.0
Women in childless couples											
Mean	56.6	+0.0	-0.0	+0.5	+0.0	-0.1	+0.2	+0.4	+0.0	+0.0	+0.0
Median	56.9	-0.0	-0.0	+0.3	+0.0	-0.1	+0.4	+0.7	+0.0	+0.0	+0.0
25th centile	48.6	-0.0	-0.1	+0.3	+0.0	+0.0	+0.3	+0.7	+0.0	+0.0	+0.0
75th centile	65.2	+0.0	+0.0	+0.4	+0.0	-0.1	+0.4	+0.3	+0.0	+0.0	+0.0
Proportion whose rate rises (%)		31.9	50.3	14.9	0.0	21.5	7.0	19.7	0.0	0.0	0.0
Proportion whose rate falls (%)		50.5	31.7	0.3	0.0	68.2	2.5	5.5	0.0	0.0	0.0

(continued)

Table 5.1: Effects of the reforms on workers' replacement rates at 40 hours (continued)

	Full-time RR before reform (%)	Change in full-time replacement rate (percentage points)									
		NI up	NI down	IS up	CB up	SRL up	HB taper down	WTC up	CTC child up	CTC big family	CTC young
Fathers in couples											
Mean	54.8	+0.1	-0.1	+1.3	+0.4	-0.1	-0.0	+0.4	+1.3	+0.4	+0.6
Median	55.1	+0.1	-0.1	+1.0	+0.4	-0.0	+0.2	+1.6	+1.7	+0.4	+0.5
25th centile	43.2	+0.1	-0.1	+0.6	+0.5	-0.0	+0.1	+1.3	+1.3	+0.3	+0.5
75th centile	66.8	+0.1	-0.1	+2.1	+0.5	-0.2	+0.5	+0.0	+1.4	+0.6	+0.7
Proportion whose rate rises (%)		92.2	2.7	58.1	99.8	18.2	8.6	45.1	89.3	17.6	38.0
Proportion whose rate falls (%)		2.7	92.2	0.0	0.2	74.9	5.4	24.2	0.3	0.1	0.7
Mothers in couples											
Mean	67.0	+0.0	-0.0	+0.4	+0.3	-0.1	+0.1	+0.8	+0.8	+0.3	+0.4
Median	67.8	+0.0	+0.0	+0.3	+0.3	-0.1	+0.2	+1.2	+0.9	+0.3	+0.4
25th centile	58.6	+0.0	-0.0	+0.2	+0.3	-0.0	+0.2	+0.9	+0.8	+0.3	+0.3
75th centile	76.0	+0.1	-0.0	+0.5	+0.3	-0.2	+0.2	+0.6	+0.9	+0.4	+0.3
Proportion whose rate rises (%)		43.2	39.0	15.9	99.7	10.9	8.4	41.2	51.3	17.2	37.6
Proportion whose rate falls (%)		39.0	43.1	0.0	0.1	81.3	3.8	10.5	0.4	0.1	0.3
All											
Mean	48.6	+0.1	-0.1	+1.9	+0.2	-0.1	-0.2	+0.0	+0.4	+0.1	+0.2
Median	50.1	+0.1	-0.1	+1.2	+0.2	-0.1	+0.2	+0.6	+0.5	+0.1	+0.2
25th centile	30.8	+0.1	-0.1	+3.1	+0.1	-0.2	+0.0	-0.2	+0.2	+0.0	+0.1
75th centile	64.9	+0.1	-0.1	+1.4	+0.2	-0.0	-0.4	-0.1	+0.7	+0.2	+0.3
Proportion whose rate rises (%)		75.0	15.3	55.6	40.8	13.6	7.1	20.1	30.6	7.0	15.1
Proportion whose rate falls (%)		15.3	74.9	0.1	0.1	79.1	8.3	18.7	0.1	0.0	0.3

Notes and sources: Authors' calculations using Family Resources Survey 2002–03 and TAXBEN under April 2005 tax and benefit system. Excludes families containing any adults aged over 55, the self-employed, or adults receiving a disability benefit. Full-time means 40 hours' work a week. NI = national insurance. IS = income support. CB = child benefit. SRL = starting-rate limit. HB = housing benefit. WTC = working tax credit. CTC = child tax credit.

Table 5.2: Effects of the reforms on workers' EMTRs

	EMTR before reform (%)	Change in EMTR (percentage points)									
		NI up	NI down	IS up	CB up	SRL up	HB taper down	WTC up	CTC child up	CTC big family	CTC young
Single people without children											
Mean	35.1	+0.5	−0.5	+0.4	+0.0	−0.2	+0.4	+1.0	+0.0	+0.0	+0.0
Median	33.0	+0.5	−0.5	+0.0	+0.0	−0.0	+0.0	+0.0	+0.0	+0.0	+0.0
25th centile	31.4	+0.5	−0.5	+0.0	+0.0	−0.0	+0.0	+0.0	+0.0	+0.0	+0.0
75th centile	33.0	+0.5	−0.5	+0.0	+0.0	+0.0	+0.0	+0.0	+0.0	+0.0	+0.0
Proportion whose rate rises (%)		92.6	0.0	1.7	0.0	0.2	4.7	3.9	0.0	0.0	0.0
Proportion whose rate falls (%)		0.0	92.7	0.1	0.0	2.7	3.1	0.4	0.0	0.0	0.0
Lone parents											
Mean	56.7	+0.4	−0.3	+1.6	+0.0	−0.3	−1.5	−1.8	+0.3	+0.0	−0.0
Median	68.4	+0.5	−0.5	+0.0	+0.0	−0.0	−0.0	−0.0	+0.0	+0.0	+0.0
25th centile	33.0	+0.5	−0.5	+0.0	+0.0	−0.0	+2.9	−0.0	+0.0	+0.0	−0.0
75th centile	70.0	+0.5	−0.5	+0.0	+0.0	+0.0	+0.0	−0.0	+0.0	+0.0	+0.0
Proportion whose rate rises (%)		64.4	0.2	10.5	0.2	0.3	13.5	5.3	2.8	0.0	0.4
Proportion whose rate falls (%)		0.4	64.4	1.5	0.0	5.6	18.2	12.5	0.3	0.0	0.2
Men in childless couples											
Mean	33.8	+0.5	−0.5	+0.1	+0.0	−0.0	+0.2	+0.7	+0.0	+0.0	+0.0
Median	33.0	+0.5	−0.5	−0.0	+0.0	+0.0	+0.0	+0.0	+0.0	+0.0	+0.0
25th centile	31.4	+0.5	−0.5	+0.0	+0.0	+0.0	+0.0	+0.0	+0.0	+0.0	+0.0
75th centile	33.0	+0.5	−0.5	+0.0	+0.0	+0.0	+0.0	+0.0	+0.0	+0.0	+0.0
Proportion whose rate rises (%)		98.6	0.0	0.5	0.0	0.1	1.6	2.3	0.0	0.0	0.0
Proportion whose rate falls (%)		0.0	98.5	0.1	0.0	0.6	0.8	0.3	0.0	0.0	0.0
Women in childless couples											
Mean	31.1	+0.4	−0.4	+0.0	+0.0	−0.2	+0.1	+0.7	+0.0	+0.0	+0.0
Median	31.4	+0.5	−0.5	−0.0	+0.0	+0.0	+0.0	+0.0	+0.0	+0.0	+0.0
25th centile	31.4	+0.5	−0.5	−0.0	+0.0	−0.0	+0.0	+0.0	+0.0	+0.0	+0.0
75th centile	33.0	+0.5	−0.5	−0.0	+0.0	+0.0	+0.0	+0.0	+0.0	+0.0	+0.0
Proportion whose rate rises (%)		88.2	0.0	0.7	0.0	0.1	1.8	2.2	0.0	0.0	0.0
Proportion whose rate falls (%)		0.0	88.2	0.2	0.0	3.2	1.0	0.3	0.0	0.0	0.0

(continued)

Table 5.2: Effects of the reforms on workers' EMTRs (continued)

	EMTR before reform (%)	Change in EMTR (percentage points)									
		NI up	NI down	IS up	CB up	SRL up	HB taper down	WTC up	CTC child up	CTC big family	CTC young
Fathers in couples											
Mean	42.0	+0.5	−0.5	+0.1	+0.0	−0.0	+0.2	+1.7	+1.1	+0.1	+0.2
Median	33.7	+0.5	−0.5	+0.0	−0.0	−0.0	+1.5	+7.7	+5.1	+0.1	+0.4
25th centile	31.4	+0.5	−0.5	−0.0	+0.0	−0.0	+0.0	+0.0	+0.0	+0.0	+0.0
75th centile	47.0	+0.5	−0.5	+0.4	+0.0	−0.0	+1.6	+4.2	+1.0	+0.7	+1.2
Proportion whose rate rises (%)		96.5	0.0	1.4	0.1	0.1	3.0	6.9	4.7	1.9	3.1
Proportion whose rate falls (%)		0.0	96.6	0.1	0.0	0.8	1.6	1.5	0.3	0.1	0.1
Mothers in couples											
Mean	33.0	+0.4	−0.4	+0.1	+0.0	−0.6	+0.2	+1.8	+1.1	+0.1	+0.2
Median	33.0	+0.5	−0.5	+0.0	+0.0	−1.6	+0.0	+0.0	+0.0	+0.0	+0.0
25th centile	31.4	+0.5	−0.5	+0.0	+0.0	−3.7	+0.0	+0.0	+0.0	+0.0	+0.0
75th centile	37.0	+0.0	−0.0	+0.0	+0.0	−0.0	+0.0	+1.1	+1.0	+0.0	+0.0
Proportion whose rate rises (%)		80.9	0.3	0.9	0.1	0.1	2.3	6.0	3.6	1.6	2.5
Proportion whose rate falls (%)		0.2	80.9	0.1	0.0	7.5	1.1	1.2	0.2	0.1	0.1
All											
Mean	36.4	+0.5	−0.5	+0.3	+0.0	−0.2	+0.2	+1.0	+0.4	+0.0	+0.1
Median	33.0	+0.5	−0.5	+0.0	+0.0	−0.0	+0.0	+0.0	+0.0	+0.0	+0.0
25th centile	31.4	+0.5	−0.5	+0.0	+0.0	−0.0	+0.0	+0.0	+0.0	+0.0	+0.0
75th centile	39.1	+0.6	−0.5	+1.5	+0.0	−0.1	+2.8	+2.8	+2.6	+0.4	+0.7
Proportion whose rate rises (%)		90.5	0.1	1.6	0.0	0.1	3.6	4.4	1.6	0.6	1.0
Proportion whose rate falls (%)		0.1	90.5	0.2	0.0	3.0	2.6	1.3	0.1	0.0	0.1

Notes and sources: Authors' calculations using Family Resources Survey 2002–03 and TAXBEN under April 2005 tax and benefit system. Excludes families containing any adults aged over 55, the self-employed, or adults receiving a disability benefit. EMTRs evaluated at usual hours worked. NI = national insurance. IS = income support. CB = child benefit. SRL = starting-rate limit. HB = housing benefit. WTC = working tax credit. CTC = child tax credit.

Table 5.3: Effects of the reforms on the distribution of workers' EMTRs between bands

EMTR (%)	Before reform	Proportion of working individuals facing EMTRs (%)									
		NI up	NI down	IS up	CB up	SRL up	HB taper down	WTC up	CTC child up	CTC big family	CTC young
0	3.12	+0.02	+0.02	−0.08	+0.00	+0.02	−0.05	−0.25	−0.10	−0.02	−0.02
0.1–10	0.61	−0.02	−0.01	−0.01	+0.00	+0.05	−0.04	+0.05	+0.01	+0.02	+0.03
10.1–20	1.39	−0.02	+0.03	−0.01	+0.00	+0.35	−0.01	−0.09	−0.03	−0.01	+0.01
20.1–30	9.20	−0.36	+0.22	+0.00	+0.00	+0.84	−0.13	−0.21	−0.10	−0.01	+0.00
30.1–40	61.24	−0.05	−0.07	−0.01	+0.04	−1.14	−1.43	−2.17	−0.65	+0.04	+0.14
40.1–50	11.94	+0.50	−0.04	+0.06	+0.01	−0.04	+0.15	+0.02	−0.01	+0.00	−0.02
50.1–60	1.37	−0.04	−0.02	−0.10	+0.00	+0.30	+2.76	+0.27	+0.04	+0.01	−0.01
60.1–70	7.83	−4.08	−0.06	−0.42	−0.02	−0.30	−0.89	+3.03	+0.88	−0.01	−0.09
70.1–80	1.03	+4.03	−0.04	+0.08	+0.00	−0.08	+0.20	−0.27	+0.01	+0.00	+0.05
80.1–90	1.36	+0.01	−0.03	+0.16	−0.01	+0.00	−0.44	−0.29	+0.00	−0.01	−0.09
90.1–100	0.68	+0.01	+0.01	+0.26	+0.00	+0.01	−0.11	−0.09	−0.01	+0.00	+0.02
Over 100	0.21	+0.00	−0.01	+0.07	−0.02	+0.00	−0.03	+0.01	−0.04	+0.00	+0.00
All	100.00	+0.00	+0.00	+0.00	+0.00	+0.00	+0.00	+0.00	+0.00	+0.00	+0.00

Notes and sources: Authors' calculations using Family Resources Survey 2002–03 and TAXBEN under April 2005 tax and benefit system. Excludes families containing any adults aged over 55, the self-employed, or adults receiving a disability benefit. EMTRs evaluated at usual hours worked. NI = national insurance. IS = income support. CB = child benefit. SRL = starting-rate limit. HB = housing benefit. WTC = working tax credit. CTC = child tax credit.

Table 5.4: Effects of the reforms on the proportion of workers with EMTRs above particular levels

| EMTR (%) | Before reform | Proportion of working individuals facing EMTRs (%) | | | | | HB taper | | CTC | CTC big | CTC |
		NI up	NI down	IS up	CB up	SRL up	down	WTC up	child up	family	young
All	100.00	+0.00	+0.00	+0.00	+0.00	+0.00	+0.00	+0.00	+0.00	+0.00	+0.00
More than 0	96.88	−0.02	−0.02	+0.08	+0.00	−0.02	+0.05	+0.25	+0.10	+0.02	+0.02
More than 10	96.27	+0.00	−0.01	+0.08	+0.00	−0.07	+0.09	+0.20	+0.09	+0.00	−0.01
More than 20	94.88	+0.02	−0.04	+0.10	+0.01	−0.42	+0.09	+0.29	+0.12	+0.02	−0.02
More than 30	85.68	+0.38	−0.26	+0.10	+0.00	−1.26	+0.22	+0.51	+0.22	+0.03	−0.01
More than 40	24.44	+0.43	−0.19	+0.11	−0.04	−0.12	+1.65	+2.68	+0.87	−0.02	−0.15
More than 50	12.50	−0.07	−0.15	+0.05	−0.05	−0.08	+1.50	+2.66	+0.89	−0.02	−0.13
More than 60	11.12	−0.03	−0.13	+0.15	−0.05	−0.38	−1.26	+2.39	+0.85	−0.02	−0.12
More than 70	3.29	+4.04	−0.07	+0.57	−0.03	−0.08	−0.37	−0.64	−0.03	−0.01	−0.02
More than 80	2.25	+0.01	−0.03	+0.49	−0.02	+0.00	−0.57	−0.37	−0.05	−0.01	−0.07
More than 90	0.89	+0.00	+0.00	+0.33	−0.02	+0.01	−0.14	−0.08	−0.05	+0.00	+0.02
More than 100	0.21	+0.00	−0.01	+0.07	−0.02	+0.00	−0.03	+0.01	−0.04	+0.00	+0.00

Notes and sources: Authors' calculations using Family Resources Survey 2002–03 and TAXBEN under April 2005 tax and benefit system. Excludes families containing any adults aged over 55, the self-employed, or adults receiving a disability benefit. EMTRs evaluated at usual hours worked. NI = national insurance. IS = income support. CB = child benefit. SRL = starting-rate limit. HB = housing benefit. WTC = working tax credit. CTC = child tax credit.

Table 5.5: Distributional effects of the reforms

Income decile group	Percentage change in net income									
	NI up	NI down	IS up	CB up	SRL up	HB taper down	WTC up	CTC child up	CTC big family	CTC young
Poorest	−0.00	0.00	9.41	0.68	0.01	0.39	0.32	1.32	0.82	0.53
2	−0.06	0.06	3.64	1.87	0.16	1.48	1.67	3.66	2.97	1.95
3	−0.19	0.20	1.35	1.37	0.45	1.41	2.92	2.56	1.82	1.49
4	−0.28	0.28	0.65	0.91	0.54	1.10	1.74	1.18	1.03	0.99
5	−0.35	0.35	0.37	0.70	0.53	0.59	0.68	0.51	0.66	0.67
6	−0.41	0.41	0.16	0.55	0.54	0.46	0.34	0.23	0.48	0.56
7	−0.45	0.45	0.08	0.44	0.50	0.38	0.19	0.10	0.32	0.57
8	−0.50	0.49	0.04	0.32	0.45	0.40	0.07	0.04	0.16	0.36
9	−0.53	0.53	0.00	0.21	0.39	0.20	0.03	0.02	0.05	0.20
Richest	−0.60	0.60	0.00	0.11	0.26	0.12	0.00	0.00	0.00	0.02

Notes and sources: Authors' calculations using Family Resources Survey 2002–03 and TAXBEN under April 2005 tax and benefit system. Excludes families containing any adults aged over 55, the self-employed, or adults receiving a disability benefit. NI = national insurance. IS = income support. CB = child benefit. SRL = starting-rate limit. HB = housing benefit. WTC = working tax credit. CTC = child tax credit.

Figure 5.1: Distributional effect – increasing NIC rates

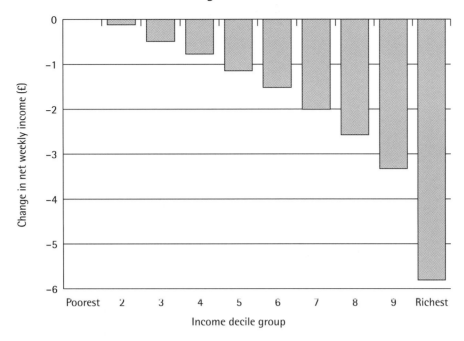

Notes and sources: Authors' calculations using Family Resources Survey 2002–03 and TAXBEN under April 2005 tax and benefit system. Excludes families containing any adults aged over 55, the self-employed, or adults receiving a disability benefit. NIC = national insurance contribution.

Figure 5.2: Distributional effect – NIC rates down, IS up, CB up

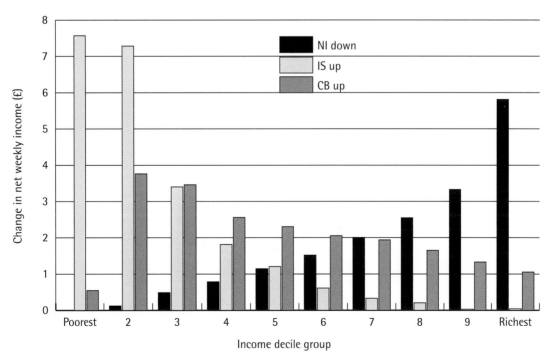

Notes and sources: Authors' calculations using Family Resources Survey 2002–03 and TAXBEN under April 2005 tax and benefit system. Excludes families containing any adults aged over 55, the self-employed, or adults receiving a disability benefit. NIC = national insurance contributions. IS = income support. CB = child benefit.

Figure 5.3: Distributional effect – SRL up, HB taper down, WTC up

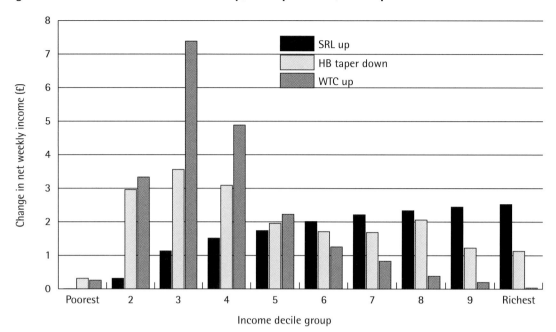

Notes and sources: Authors' calculations using Family Resources Survey 2002–03 and TAXBEN under April 2005 tax and benefit system. Excludes families containing any adults aged over 55, the self-employed, or adults receiving a disability benefit. SRL = starting-rate limit. HB = housing benefit. WTC = working tax credit.

Figure 5.4: Distributional effect – CTC child up, CTC big-family premium, CTC young-child premium

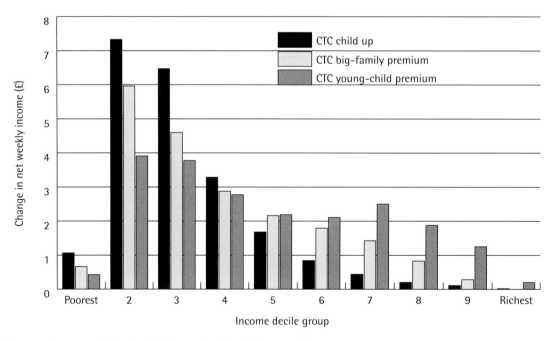

Notes and sources: Authors' calculations using Family Resources Survey 2002–03 and TAXBEN under April 2005 tax and benefit system. Excludes families containing any adults aged over 55, the self-employed, or adults receiving a disability benefit. CTC = child tax credit.

Table 5.6: Summary of the effects of the reforms

Reform	Direct effect on income distribution	Effect on full-time replacement rates	Effect on EMTRs
NI up	Progressive: rich lose most	Small rise for most, but falls for some people with working partners	Moderate rise for almost everyone
NI down	Regressive: rich gain most	Small fall for most, but rises for some people with working partners	Moderate fall for almost everyone
IS up	Exceptionally progressive: big gains for poorest	Massive rise for all except for two-earner couples	Big rise for a few, fairly small rise on average
CB up	Moderately progressive	Fairly small rise on average: moderate rise for parents, non-parents unaffected	Negligible
SRL up	Rich gain most in cash terms, middle-income families in percentage terms	Small fall for most, but rises for some	Small fall on average, big for some
HB taper down	Weakly progressive	Complicated and mixed	Mixed: highest EMTRs fall but lower ones rise; rise on average
WTC up	Moderately progressive	Mixed: falls for many without working partners, but rises for many with working partners	Big rise on average, but falls for a few
CTC child up	Extremely progressive	Moderate rise on average: big rise for most parents, non-parents unaffected	Moderate rise on average, big for a few
CTC big family	Very progressive	Small rise on average: big rise for those with large families, others unaffected	Negligible
CTC young	Moderately progressive	Fairly small rise on average: big rise for those with young children, others unaffected	Negligible

Notes: NI = national insurance. IS = income support. CB = child benefit. SRL = starting-rate limit. HB = housing benefit. WTC = working tax credit. CTC = child tax credit.

6

Conclusion

The natural conflict between redistributing income and strengthening financial work incentives raises crucial questions of policy for all governments to address. Yet while there has been a great deal of research analysing and explaining trends in poverty and inequality, very little has been done to quantify work incentives in a similar way, or to examine in detail the relationship between work incentives and redistribution in Britain. This report looks at the distribution of work incentives in Britain, what has driven changes in this distribution between 1979 and 2006, and how these trends compare with trends in poverty and inequality. The report also looks at how various policy options for the future affect both the income distribution directly and the distribution of work incentives.

Patterns in work incentives

We distinguish between two types of work incentive: the incentive to be in work at all, and the incentive to progress in work (that is, to increase earnings – whether by working longer hours, seeking promotion or moving job). In both cases, the weakest incentives are today created not by higher rates of income tax, but by the withdrawal of means-tested benefits and tax credits.

Lone parents have the weakest work incentives of the six demographic groups we consider. This is true even before taking account of childcare costs, which substantially weaken work incentives for lone parents and for second earners in couples. Since lone parents are also the poorest demographic group and since their number has more than doubled since 1979, they should be a key focus for policy makers' attention.

Financial work incentives have strengthened on average since 1979. This trend has not been consistent, however. Incentives to work at all strengthened over most of the 1980s and most of the 1990s, but weakened at the turn of the 1980s, the turn of the 1990s and the early 2000s. Incentives to progress strengthened in the second half of the 1980s and the second half of the 1990s, but weakened in the first half of the 1980s, the first half of the 1990s and at the start of the 2000s.

Only part of these changes in work incentives are the direct result of tax and benefit reforms: changes in average wages, wage inequality and rent levels are also important explanatory factors. Separating out these various factors, we find that real tax and benefit changes since 1979 have strengthened work incentives on average, although the precise trends vary by family type. Overall, changes under the Conservatives acted to strengthen average work incentives – despite weakening them for a period in the early 1980s – whereas Labour's reforms to date have weakened financial work incentives on average: since 1999, tax and benefit changes have increased the average EMTR by almost three percentage points.

Work incentives and income redistribution

While financial work incentives have strengthened on average since 1979, poverty and inequality have increased. Often they have seemed to move in step, work incentives strengthening most in years when poverty and inequality rose most.

However, this should not simply be interpreted as the redistribution–work incentives trade-off in action. That ignores the complicated effects that people's responses to work incentives may have on poverty and inequality. More importantly, many things other than tax and benefit policy also affect work incentives and the income distribution, and these things have also changed since 1979. Indeed, decomposition analyses appear to show that real tax and benefit changes alone acted both to strengthen work incentives *and* to reduce poverty and inequality – although it would be equally naïve to conclude that no policy trade-off exists. There are simply too many complications and conflicting influences at work to draw firm conclusions about the policy trade-off from broad historical trends.

Simulations of particular reforms can be more informative about the policy trade-off. In this report, we simulate tax cuts – which strengthen work incentives but do little to help the poor directly – increases in means-tested benefits and tax credits – which help the poor a lot but also damage work incentives – and increases in non-means-tested benefits – which damage work incentives less but also support the poor less. The only changes that unambiguously strengthen work incentives are also unambiguously regressive: tax cuts that give more to the rich than the poor, or benefit cuts that take more from the poor than the rich.

These broad qualitative findings are quite predictable. Some of our simulations – increasing WTC, for example, or reducing the housing benefit taper rate – yield less obvious results. Nevertheless, our main contribution in this respect is to quantify and compare the effects of different reforms, to delineate a set of feasible points in the policy trade-off. To draw normative conclusions for policy, more input is needed.

In this report, we do not attempt to estimate how much people respond to work incentives. This is clearly vital for policy: is 'helping people to help themselves' more or less effective than just helping them directly? There is not necessarily a one-dimensional answer to this. Different groups may respond in different ways, so that the right tax and benefit system to apply to lone parents may be different from that for couples without children. People's responsiveness to a tax cut will also depend on the baseline tax rate: cuts from 90% to 80% are likely to induce a bigger response than cuts from 40% to 30%. The magnitude of this difference is important when evaluating a reduction in the housing benefit taper rate, for example, where the choice is between leaving a few people with very weak work incentives or leaving many more people with fairly weak work incentives. Because people's responsiveness affects the revenue gain or cost of reforms, it even determines the set of options that are available. It is possible that a tax cut (particularly for a highly responsive group that currently faces high tax rates) might encourage work to such an extent that it pays for itself: this is the famous 'Laffer curve' effect. Many other studies do estimate people's responsiveness to tax changes; Adam (2005) analyses what can be said about the trade-off for two simple reforms once we specify people's responsiveness.

Even more fundamentally, however, policy conclusions require a set of social preferences. Does society or the government care more about particular family types (such as those with children)? Is the priority to help the very poorest at all costs to the rest of society, or to help those most easily helped without doing too much damage to others? Even if cutting benefits pushes lots of people into work and therefore reduces the number in poverty, is it worth the cost to those who are left behind in even more abject poverty?

It was not our role in this report to espouse some set of social goals. But that is something all governments must do, implicitly if not explicitly, and we can draw some conclusions from the government's statements and actions. For example, the government has adopted specific *child* poverty targets, but no such targets for working-age adults without children. This means that there is the potential both to increase direct support and strengthen work incentives for parents, but this must come at the cost of weakening the trade-off for those without children. And the government has indeed undertaken major redistribution from people without children to people with children.

Government policy and the incentives–redistribution trade-off

The government has both a poverty agenda and a 'make work pay' agenda. It has set targets to reduce child poverty from its 1998–99 level by a quarter by 2004–05 and by half by 2009–10, and to 'eradicate' it by 2020. The government also has an aim to abolish pensioner poverty, but it has made no explicit statement indicating a concern with income inequality as such.

On 'making work pay', the government argues that its strategy is designed to tackle both the 'unemployment trap' (weak incentives to work at all) and the 'poverty trap' (weak incentives to progress in work) (HM Treasury, 2003, p 9). Its targets, though, relate specifically to employment rates: the government has targets to increase the overall working-age employment rate (by an unspecified amount) between 2005 and 2008,[18] and to increase the employment rate for certain disadvantaged groups by more than this amount.[19] In February 2005, the Department for Work and Pension's (DWP) Five Year Strategy stated an aspiration to raise the working-age employment rate to 80% (from around 75% now) (DWP, 2005, p 4), although at the time of writing no target date has yet been set.

Two groups that are particularly important for this government agenda are neglected in this report. One is people claiming incapacity benefits. Incapacity benefits are currently in the process of reform: the government is piloting Pathways to Work reforms in a number of areas, and its Welfare Reform Bill, published in July 2006, proposes not only to roll out the Pathways to Work reforms nationwide but also to introduce more fundamental reform of incapacity benefits.[20] It is looking for employment growth in this group more than in any other. To achieve its aspiration of an 80% employment rate, it reckons that 2.5 million more people need to be in work (DWP, 2005, p 26). The government hopes that 1 million of these will come from those who are on incapacity benefits (by 2016), compared with a target of moving 0.3 million lone parents into work (by 2010) (DWP, 2006b, p 4).

The second important group we neglect is older workers and pensioners. As well as the aim of abolishing pensioner poverty mentioned above, the government has focused strongly on keeping older workers in the labour market. However, our work excludes both the over-55s and incapacity benefit recipients, because their work incentives are difficult to model and their working decisions raise rather different issues from the main subject of this report. Our findings, then, relate to the rest of the working-age population.

---

[18] This is a joint HMT and DWP Public Service Agreement target; see HM Treasury (2004).

[19] DWP Public Service Agreement target 4; see HM Treasury (2004).

[20] The text of the bill is at www.publications.parliament.uk/pa/cm200506/cmbills/208/2006208.pdf

The government argues that its 'make work pay' agenda reinforces its poverty agenda: that the best way to reduce poverty is to move people into work. This labour market approach to reducing poverty is clearly one on which the government intends to focus: as part of its objective of reducing child poverty, the DWP has a Public Service Agreement sub-target to reduce the proportion of children in workless households by 5% between spring 2005 and spring 2008. As mentioned above, the government also aims to move 300,000 more lone parents into work by 2010, bringing this group's employment rate up to 70%.

Encouraging people into work clearly would help to reduce poverty. But one cannot ignore the other side of the problem: the difficulty of incentivising work without making worklessness more unpleasant and thereby worsening poverty for those who remain out of work. The most obvious tool the government has for trying to do this is WTC. But while increasing WTC would encourage the first person in a family to work, it would discourage them from progressing further. Similarly, reducing benefit and tax credit taper rates helps people to progress to a certain point, but then discourages them from progressing further. Lowering taper rates and increasing in-work support carry a real risk of moving people above the poverty line but then leaving vast swathes of them barely above that level. That may or may not be better than the alternatives; but if such outcomes help to meet poverty targets, that is partly a reflection of the deficiencies of headcount measures of poverty.

However, the government's main weapon for fighting child poverty so far has not been such labour market measures. The most striking reforms have been increases in the child element of the CTC (and its predecessors): continual large increases have meant that its value has more than doubled in real terms since Labour came to power in 1997. This trend runs precisely counter to the labour market approach described above: it provides closely targeted support to reduce child poverty, but at the cost of damaging work incentives. The recent re-emphasis on encouraging work as a route to reducing poverty in the Five Year Strategy may signal that the government has recognised that simply increasing aggressively means-tested support indefinitely is not a sustainable strategy for reducing poverty, and may even be counterproductive. But any new emphasis on work incentives is yet to show up in tax and benefit policy: in the 2006 Budget, the Chancellor pledged to increase the child element of the CTC at least in line with average earnings growth each year up to and including 2009–10, and the threshold of the WTC is still frozen, reducing its value in real terms.

Our simulations have highlighted the attractions of an alternative approach. Since having young children or three or more children are excellent indicators of poverty, providing support to these families that is only weakly related to income can do a great deal to reduce poverty while doing very little damage to work incentives. This approach does have potential disadvantages – it can introduce issues of fairness between different family types and change fertility incentives, for example – and it is a promising avenue for future research.

An important part of Labour's first-term programme was the introduction of the 10% income tax band, which it claimed would both help those on low incomes and strengthen work incentives; Labour's 2001 general election manifesto pledged to extend the 10% band. In fact, our simulations demonstrate that such an extension would not be a particularly good way of helping those on low incomes, and its effect on work incentives would be limited. This might explain why this reform seems to have dropped off the agenda: the 2001 manifesto pledge went unfulfilled and was not repeated in 2005.

One clue to future policy reforms might come from some of the pilots that are currently being run by the DWP. In particular, the Employment, Retention and Advancement demonstration, the In-Work Credit, and the Return to Work Credit in Pathways to Work each provide very generous support to people who move from welfare to work – substantially strengthening the financial reward to work – but they only provide support for narrowly defined groups, and only for a limited period of time: they are intended to act as temporary support that hopefully leads to permanent changes in behaviour. These three pilots may indicate an increased willingness to make use of time limits, and of much more precise targeting, in designing make-work-pay policies – something that has been done a lot more in the US and Canada, for example.[21]

The people with the worst incentives to progress in work are those facing withdrawal of housing benefit, tax credits, or both. In 1999 the government took one step towards solving this by replacing family credit with working families' tax credit, which was withdrawn less sharply with income. However, a basic-rate taxpayer paying standard-rate national insurance contributions and facing withdrawal of both tax credits and housing benefit still stands to lose 89.5p of each extra £1 earned – indeed, they lose 95.5p if they also face withdrawal of council tax benefit.

Cutting the taper rate for housing benefit would reduce these punitive effective marginal tax rates (EMTRs) and would be very much in keeping with the tax credit reform of 1999. However, the problem with such measures is that they float many more people onto means-tests, and therefore increase the number of people facing quite high EMTRs much more than they reduce the number facing the very highest EMTRs. This has been the effect of Labour's policies to date, and it would be an important consequence of reducing the housing benefit taper rate: reducing the taper from 65% to 36.1% would reduce by 170,000 the number of people losing more than 60p of each extra £1 earned, but it would increase the number losing 50–60p by 440,000. It is a difficult balance to strike and perhaps explains why, despite long being identified as a major source of disincentives to work, the structure of the housing benefit means-test remains essentially unreformed since its introduction in 1988.

The DWP Five Year Strategy recognises that 'the current structure and operation of housing benefit can still be a disincentive to work' (DWP, 2005, p 29), but the reforms that the government is implementing – simplifying procedures and introducing a 'local housing allowance,' which is unrelated to actual rent – do not address the high effective tax rates that housing benefit creates. Tackling this remains one of the key issues for the government if it is serious about strengthening financial work incentives as a means to alleviating poverty.

---

[21] See Gregg et al (2006) or Grogger and Karoly (2005).

References

Adam, S. (2005) 'Measuring the marginal efficiency cost of redistribution in the UK', Institute for Fiscal Studies Working Papers W05/14.

Adam, S. and Brewer, M. (2004) *Supporting Families: The Financial Costs and Benefits of Children since 1975*, Bristol: The Policy Press.

Adam, S., Brewer, M. and Shephard, A. (2006) 'Financial work incentives in Britain: comparisons over time and between family types', forthcoming as Institute for Fiscal Studies Working Paper.

Adelman, L., Middleton, S. and Ashworth, K. (2003) *Britain's Poorest Children: Severe and Persistent Poverty and Social Exclusion*, London: Save the Children.

Akerlof, G. (1978) 'The economics of 'tagging' as applied to the optimal income tax, welfare programs, and manpower planning', *American Economic Review*, no 68, pp 8–19.

Blundell, R. (2002) 'Welfare-to-work: which policies work and why?', Keynes Lecture in Economics, *Proceedings of The British Academy*, vol 117, pp 477–524.

Bradshaw, J., Finch, N., Mayhew, E., Veli-Matti, R. and Skinner, C. (2006) *Child Poverty in Large Families*, Bristol/York: The Policy Press/Joseph Rowntree Foundation.

Brewer, M. and Clark, T. (2002) 'Social security reforms and incentives', Paper presented at Institute for Fiscal Studies conference Social Security Policy under New Labour, London, May (available as IFS Working Paper 02/14).

Brewer, M. and Shephard, A. (2004) *Did Labour Make Work Pay?*, York: Joseph Rowntree Foundation.

Brewer, M., Browne, J. and Sutherland, H. (2006a), 'Micro-simulating child poverty in 2010 and 2020', forthcoming as Joseph Rowntree Foundation Working Paper (www.jrf.org.uk/child-poverty/what-we-are-doing.asp; last accessed April 2006).

Brewer, M., Clark, T. and Goodman, A. (2003) 'What really happened to child poverty in the UK under Labour's first term?', *Economic Journal*, vol 113, pp F240–57.

Brewer, M., Goodman, A. and Leicester, A. (2006b) *Household Spending in Britain: What Does it Tell us About Poverty?*, Bristol: The Policy Press.

Brewer, M., Duncan, A., Shephard, A. and Suárez, M. (2005) 'Did Working Families' Tax Credit work? The final evaluation of the impact of in-work support on parents' labour supply and take-up behaviour in the UK', Inland Revenue Working Paper 2 (www.hmrc.gov.uk/research/ifs-laboursupply.pdf; last accessed April 2006).

Brewer, M., Goodman, A., Shaw, J. and Sibieta, L. (2006c) *Poverty and Inequality in Britain*, London: Institute for Fiscal Studies.

Clark, T. and Leicester, A. (2004) 'Inequality and two decades of British tax and benefit reform', *Fiscal Studies*, vol 25, no 2, pp 129–58.

Dickens, R. and Ellwood, D. (2003) 'Child poverty in Britain and the United States', *Economic Journal*, vol 113, no 488, pp F219–F239.

DWP (Department for Work and Pensions) (2005) *Five Year Strategy: Opportunity and Security Throughout Life*, Cm 6447, Norwich: The Stationery Office.

DWP (2006a) *Households Below Average Income 1994/95–2004/05*, Leeds: Corporate Document Services.

DWP (2006b) *A New Deal for Welfare: Empowering People to Work*, Cm 6730, Norwich: The Stationery Office.

Evans, M. and Eyre, J. (2004) *The Opportunities of a Lifetime: Model Lifetime Analysis of Current British Social Policy*, Bristol: The Policy Press.

Goodman, A., Johnson, J. and Webb, S. (1997) *Inequality in the UK*, Oxford: Oxford University Press.

Gregg, P., Harkness, S. and Macmillan, L. (2006) 'Welfare to work policies and child poverty: a review of issues relating to the labour market and economy, particularly in terms of the impact of labour market initiatives on children's income poverty', forthcoming as Joseph Rowntree Foundation Working Paper (www.jrf.org.uk/child-poverty/what-we-are-doing.asp; last accessed April 2006)

Grogger, J. and Karoly, L. (2005) *Welfare Reform: Effects of a Decade of Change*, Cambridge, MA: Harvard University Press.

HM Treasury (2003) *Full Employment in Every Region*, London: HM Treasury.

HM Treasury (2004) *2004 Spending review: Public Service Agreements 2005–2008*, London: The Stationery Office.

HM Treasury (2005 and previous years) *Tax Ready Reckoner and Tax Reliefs*, London: HM Treasury.

HM Treasury (2006) *Budget 2006: A Strong and Strengthening Economy: Investing in Britain's Future*, HC 96, London: The Stationery Office.

Jones, F. (2005) *The Effects of Taxes and Benefits on Household Income, 2003–04*, London: Office for National Statistics.

Mirrlees, J.A. (1971) 'An exploration in the theory of optimal income taxation', *Review of Economic Studies*, vol 38, no 2, pp 175–208.

Sutherland, H., Sefton, T. and Piachaud, D. (2003) *Poverty in Britain*, York: Joseph Rowntree Foundation.

Appendix

Much of our analysis is based on measures of net incomes and work incentives produced by the Institute for Fiscal Studies' tax and benefit micro-simulation model, TAXBEN. This is able to calculate accurate budget constraints, and therefore measures of financial work incentives.

This Appendix gives brief details of the analysis of financial work incentives, and summarises material in Adam et al (2006).

Data

TAXBEN is able to use data from the Family Resources Survey (FRS) and the Family Expenditure Survey (FES). The FRS is an annual cross-section survey of 27,000 households in Britain, and began in 1994. The FES is an annual cross-section survey of around 7,000 households in the UK, available from the 1960s through to 2000/01. The analysis uses the FES until 1993, and the FRS between 1994/95 and 2002/03. Years refer to calendar years until 1993, and then financial years. Synthetic data for 2003/04 to 2005/06 was created by uprating data from 2002/03, as described in Brewer et al (2006a).

The analysis of work incentives in this report is restricted to working individuals in families in which no one is aged over 55 or receiving a disability benefit. Individuals with particularly complicated budget constraints, who did not have an hourly wage or who had extreme values of measures of work incentives were also omitted from the analysis. Details of the final samples used are available from the authors.

Net income

Net income is income after deducting direct taxes on income, and adding income from state benefits and tax credits. It does not take account of indirect taxes. Nor do our measures of work incentives take account of taxes formally incident on employers, such as employers' national insurance contributions (NICs); this could be done by adding employers' NICs back into gross income. Ideally, micro-simulation estimates of work incentives would incorporate non-take-up of benefits and tax credits, but our need for a consistent approach over 25 years means we opted to assume full take-up. The direction of bias that this will impart to our results depends on the detail of the particular means-tested benefit/tax credit.

People who work have to incur important work-related costs, such as for clothing, transport and childcare. Information on these costs is not usually collected in household surveys, making it difficult to incorporate them into our micro-simulation analysis. Data are available, however, on childcare expenditures. Deducting this expenditure from the measure of net income while working makes a considerable difference to the estimated work incentives of parents, but we do not follow this approach. This is partly because some parents spend money on childcare for non-work-related reasons, meaning that it would be wrong to assume that childcare expenditure would not be incurred were parents not to work. Second, one of the surveys we use (the FES) does not have such rich data on childcare costs as other surveys that now exist.

Net income is defined at the family level: this means that, when comparing the income in and out of work for an individual in a couple, we will include in the calculations the net earnings of the partner.

The 'margin' used when calculating effective marginal tax rates

The empirical analysis in this report calculates effective marginal tax rates (EMTRs) by increasing weekly hours by 5% (approximately an hour a week for someone working part time, and two hours a week for someone working full time). EMTRs estimated in this way will be identical to those calculated by increasing the hourly wage by 5% except where there are hours rules in the means-tested benefits and tax credit system. Adam et al (2006) examine the implications of using a larger margin to calculate EMTRs.

The time period considered when measuring net income

The main analysis in this report is based on a long-run measure of net income (and therefore financial work incentives), where we ignore the income disregard in the new tax credits, assume that no one is entitled to contribution-based jobseeker's allowance and allow home-owners to receive mortgage interest payments if they are entitled to income support or income-based jobseeker's allowance. Adam et al (2006) explore the implications of using a short-run measure of income.

All the work incentive measures discussed require us to specify the individual's wage. If we limit our analysis to those individuals who are working, then this presents no problems, as we can use the wage reported in the household survey data. For non-working individuals this is clearly not possible. Difficulties in consistently estimating the wages that would be earned by people observed to be not working in our data over 25 years mean that the analysis focuses on the incentive to work for those observed in work; Adam et al (2006) show some estimates of the incentive to work for those not in work.